ALL
I COULD
BARE
...

ALSO BY CRAIG SEYMOUR

Luther:
The Life and Longing of Luther Vandross

ALL
I COULD
BARE

• • •

My Life in the Strip Clubs
of Gay Washington, D.C.

• • •

CRAIG SEYMOUR

ATRIA BOOKS

New York   London   Toronto   Sydney

ATRIA BOOKS

A Division of Simon & Schuster, Inc.
1230 Avenue of the Americas
New York, NY 10020

Copyright © 2008 by Craig Seymour

First Atria Books hardcover edition June 2008

ATRIA BOOKS and colophon are trademarks
of Simon & Schuster, Inc.

For information about special discounts for bulk purchases,
please contact Simon & Schuster Special Sales at
1-800-456-6798 or business@simonandschuster.com.

Manufactured in the United States of America

10   9   8   7   6   5   4   3   2   1

Library of Congress Cataloging-in-Publication Data

Seymour, Craig.
All I could bare: my life in the strip clubs of gay Washington, D.C. /
Craig Seymour.—1st Atria Books hardcover ed.
p. cm.
1. Seymour, Craig. 2. Gay men—Washington (D.C.)—
Biography. 3. Male strippers—Washington (D.C.)—
Biography. I. Title.

HQ75.8.S47A3 2008
306.77092—dc22
[B]
2007043446

ISBN-13: 978-1-4165-4205-6
ISBN-10:   1-4165-4205-1

To Seth—
This story is yours as much as mine. Thanks for always
making me feel like I could do anything.

Freedom means the opportunity to be
what we never thought we would be.

—Daniel J. Boorstin

On what strange circumstances
are whole lives changed.

—Bette Davis

All of the stories and experiences in this book are true, based upon the memory of actual events. I have made no embellishments or distortions for dramatic effect. However, in order to protect the anonymity of certain people who probably never expected—or wanted—to have their strip club experiences immortalized in a book, I have created a few composite characters and changed the names and identifying characteristics of a small number of others.

Prologue

• • •

So, you used to be a stripper?" he asks.

I'm on a date at a bar in Providence, Rhode Island, where I live. It's my first date in months. OK, more than a year. The guy is cute in that dorky way I like. He reads books, has lived in New York. I really want this to work. I really want a kiss.

"Yeah, back in D.C., when I was in grad school," I answer.

"You danced around and spun on poles and stuff?"

"Not exactly," I say. "Mostly I just stood there and let people play with my dick."

His jaw perceptibly drops.

I continue: "See, D.C. used to have some of the wildest strip clubs in the country, surprisingly enough. Customers could basically stroke our dicks and feel us up, and they'd always try to stick their fingers up our asses."

"That doesn't sound legal," he says, mouth in a suspicious smirk.

"No one really knew if it was legal or not. But it had been going on for years and the cops sorta turned a blind eye. It's different now. But that's how it was when *I* danced."

"It's hard to believe this happened in our nation's capital," he says, taking a swig from his PBR.

"I know, right. But you have to remember that the mayor was on crack most of this time."

He nods in an "I never thought of that" kind of way.

"So, why'd you do it?" he asks.

I knew this was coming. It's the inevitable question, the first part of what I've unaffectionately come to call the interro-gogo. It's when people try to figure out if my reasons for stripping jibe with their notions—often informed by TV movies, newsmagazine exposés, and daytime talk shows—about why people strip. This line of inquiry alternately makes me want to fight or crawl beneath the nearest throw rug.

Because of this, I keep things simple.

"It was just something I'd always wanted to try," I say.

He kind of smiles, and though I don't know why, it relaxes me.

"Did you feel used with all those guys pawing on you?"

"Sometimes, yeah; but most times, no. And it certainly wasn't the first or last time I'd ever felt used at a job. But generally it was a lot of fun. It was all about doing something that was a little unexpected and out there, you know?"

"So, how'd you start?"

"Well, it was sorta like this . . ."

1

F uck it." The words whipped through my head
as I stood in the cold hallway with my hand on
the door leading to the stage. A sign on the door
read: THIS IS NOT AN EXIT. The music thumped loudly—
all beats, whooshes, and wails, like a gospel diva trapped
in a washing machine. I took a rushed breath, twisted the
doorknob, and walked inside, going from the sunshine of
the hallway to the midnight of the theater.

I couldn't see a thing, not really. It took what seemed like
a full minute for my eyes to adjust to the darkness of the
brick room painted black. I started to make out the outlines
of figures seated in the rows of seats in front of the stage
and standing along the back wall. The music continued to
thump, louder now that I was inside, and the air smelled
of Clorox and crotch. Beads of chilly sweat dripped from
my armpits. My heartbeat quickened. Again those words,
"Fuck it."

I started up the steps toward the stage and positioned myself in front of a large hanging screen that minutes earlier had been showing the fuzzy projected images of two California surfer dudes fucking by a pool. Once I made it to center stage, the D.J. in the overhead booth switched on the spotlight. I was now burning in a hard white sun.

Dressed in a too-tight T-shirt and shredded, hanging-off-my-ass jean shorts, I looked like the slutty boy at summer camp, the one who frequently disappears with the artsy male counselors. People were always telling me how young I looked, so I thought the camp thing worked for me.

Before my eyes could get used to the spotlight, the D.J. bellowed over the loudspeaker in a seventies game show announcer voice, "Gentlemen, welcome to the Follies. Our next dancer is making his first appearance here. Put your hands together for . . . [long dramatic pause] Craig."

"This is it," I thought. "There's no putting your khakis back on now." I stood there and started to dance a little bit, moving my feet from side to side with great deliberateness, like the gangly boys at the high school dance. Fortunately, there were no Chippendales-like dance routines needed here. It wasn't that kind of place. The guys who came to the Follies—Washington, D.C.'s oldest gay porn theater and, if you believed their ads, home of the hottest "all male burlesque"—wanted flesh and they wanted it fast. This was less striptease than strip-touch. The dancer's job was to get onstage, disrobe quickly, try to get a hard-on, and then walk out among the customers, who for a tip—generally a buck—got to stroke, fondle, poke, and prod the dancer's bod. It was more like sex than dancing, and it had become my job.

This was quite a change for me, since I spent most of my days as a graduate student and teacher at the University of Maryland in College Park: going to classes, giving lectures, grading papers, all on a campus so idyllic and grassy that it was used as the school in *St. Elmo's Fire.* But I was ready for a change. I *needed* it even if I couldn't explain exactly why.

I knew I was taking a risk by dancing here. The Follies itself could be a dangerous place. A 1977 fire took eight lives, among them a congressional aide, a Midwestern minister, an ex-marine, and an economist for the World Bank. Then, fifteen years later, more than a dozen flashlight-wielding cops stormed into the dark theater and arrested fourteen men on sodomy and other sex-related charges. Three dancers got caught up in the sweep. One guy, wearing only cowboy boots, was busted in the middle of his set.

I also was taking a risk because I wasn't sure what would happen if the people at school, especially my students or, even worse, their parents, found out about it.

But I didn't really care about these risks. I couldn't afford to. It was a journey I felt compelled to take—the road less clothed—and this was my first step.

As I stood there onstage, the wailing diva song played on. I knew I had to start taking something off, but I didn't really know *how* to do it. Like most people, I'd never given much thought to taking off my clothes. It was just something I did. But now I had an audience that was expecting me to do it, and it wasn't like there was a training course or apprenticeship program for aspiring strippers.

First I lifted up my T-shirt, gripping it from the bottom and pulling it inside out over my head. (I'd later find out that this was the girly way of taking off a shirt; a real man grabs it from the back of the collar and pulls it over his head.) Once my chest was bare, I sucked in my stomach and felt my nipples harden in the cold air.

Next I took off my jean shorts, first playing with the front snap, then slowly lowering the zipper and letting the denim drop. I wasn't wearing any underwear, because no self-respecting summer camp boy-slut wears drawers. Then I stepped out of the shorts, one leg at a time. I was now entirely naked, except for my sneakers and two white tube socks on my feet. My grandmother had given me these socks for Christmas a few months before, and I really liked them because they had dark gray patches at the toe and heel.

The next thing I had to worry about was my dick. It wasn't hard. It was even a little shrunken from the cold. I started tugging on it nervously. I didn't know what to do. When I jerked off at home, I was usually lying down watching a porn tape or flipping through a magazine, not standing upright in front of a room of strangers. I probably should've been thinking about something that turned me on, but my mind wasn't really working that way. I wasn't actually having thoughts. It was all a nervous rush.

I kept yanking on my dick. Hours, years, a full millennium seemed to pass. I tugged some more until I finally got it to a respectable hang. Once again I thought, "Fuck it," and headed out into the audience, walking down from the stage, carefully taking one step at a time.

I stood in front of the rows of seats and instantly felt safer. It was dark here, away from the spotlight of the stage. My heart rate slowed.

There was no one in the first two rows, which had several broken seats covered with duct tape, so I walked over to an older guy in the third row. He smiled as I stood in front of him and lifted my left leg, propping it on one of his armrests. He placed a folded dollar bill into my sock and put one hand firmly behind my balls, using the other hand to grab my dick. I got rock hard as he moved his hand back and forth. I couldn't explain why. It wasn't like he was hot or anything, and I could even make out a bit of old guy smell beneath the general Follies funk. But here I was, as hard as I'd ever been. It wasn't so much what the guy was doing to me as the fact that, after thinking about it for a long time, I was really doing this.

I stayed with him for about a minute. In my mind, I imagined a parking meter. I was wondering how much time he should get for a buck. My set lasted only ten minutes and there were about six other customers I had to get to.

I slowly pulled away from him, leaned over, and whispered, "Thank you."

"No," he responded. "Thank *you.*"

I smiled and moved to my next customer, another older white dude, who asked, "What are you?" as he grabbed my package.

"Excuse me?"

"What are you? What nationality?"

"Um, American, the last time I checked my passport."

"I mean, what's your ethnic background? You look Hispanic or Filipino or something."

At the clubs, most of the dancers were white, with the occasional black, Latino, or I-dunno–looking guy like me thrown in. It made for some interesting conversations as customers tried to figure out if who you were matched who they wanted you to be.

"I'm black," I aid.

"Really? You don't look it." I shrugged my shoulders.

"Is one of your parents white?" he asked.

"Nope."

"Oh, well, you have an interesting look."

"Thanks," I said, adding in my mind, "I guess."

I left this guy and moved on to the next customer, who sat in the back row. He was an Asian guy in his twenties. I positioned myself in front of him, my dick still at full mast.

"That looks dangerous," he said as he put some bills in my sock and started stroking me. "What is it, about ten inches?"

"I don't know," I said. "I've never measured it." I really hadn't.

His head lowered and his eyes fixed on my dick like it was some kind of target. Then he pulled on it with all his might like he was in a yanking contest at the county fair.

"Whoa, man. Slow down," I said. "Jeez."

I put my hand over his and moved it slowly back and forth.

"Like this," I said. He looked up sheepishly and gave me another tip.

With my time almost over, I made my way to the last guy in the back row, who was by far the weirdest. He was short and fat, with pale, pasty skin and a few shellacked wisps of hair plastered to his nearly bald scalp. When I stood in front of him, he tipped me and then reached for my dick with his thumb and forefinger like he was examining something in a laboratory. ("A human male penis. Interesting. Notice its firmness and veiny texture.") His clinical manner made my cock deflate instantly like a whoopee cushion underneath a fat ass.

"You can tell a lot about how a guy masturbates by the way he touches you," said Casey, one of the two other dancers I was working with, after I finished my set. We were sitting in the dressing room—which was also a functioning broom closet—waiting for the finale, where we all danced together. I used the time to debrief.

"Some of them are just plain weird, though," I said, "and then this one guy pulled it so hard that it was like he wanted to take it home as a souvenir. My dick felt like one of those metal handles that people hold on to while riding the subway."

Casey laughed and told me to buy a tube of Elbow Grease, a creamy, oil-based lubricant, from the front counter. "It helps cut down on the wear and tear," he explained, rubbing lotion over his arms, which had tattoos curling down them like colorful snakes.

We waited in the dressing room while the other dancer went through his set, then we went back to the theater for the ten-minute finale. I don't remember any of the other songs that played while I was dancing, but the last song of the finale was Madonna's "Where's the Party."

As I walked through the audience again—butt naked, hands on my dick, Madonna thumping in my ear ("Where's the party, I want to free my soul / Where's the party, I want to lose control")—I felt that I'd made a transformation as surely as Superman slipping out of a phone booth or Wonder Woman doing a sunburst spin. I was bare-ass in a room of paying strangers, a stripper. After years of wondering what it would be like, I had done it—faced a fear, defied expectation, embraced a taboo self. It was only the beginning.

2

I first went to one of D.C.'s gay strip clubs as a customer. It was summer 1990 and I'd read in the local gay paper that my favorite porn star, Joey Stefano, was appearing at La Cage Aux Follies, one of the oldest gay strip joints in the city. For me, Joey was less a cheesy porn dude than a genuine XXX role model.

See, Joey was the guy who made me feel it was OK to have—and even possibly enjoy—gay sex, butt-fucking specifically. I was still a marginally closeted gay-sex virgin. (Sweet twenty-one and never been reamed.) But watching Joey get his smooth, tan, perfectly rounded rump plowed on the small screen made me feel like I could actually do this whole gay thing. I knew I had the emotional attachment stuff down, as heart-wrenching crushes on some high school friends had proved; and that year I'd even found the courage to come out to my mom and dad. But the idea of gay sex had always freaked me out, especially since I came of age in the eighties, when AIDS hysteria was at full tilt. It was, therefore, reassuring to see that someone like Joey could get fucked in the ass without succumbing to an instant pestilence-filled death or having his lower intestine fall out in a bloody coil.

There was no way I was going to miss seeing Joey once I found out he was coming to town. But the idea of going to a gay strip club scared the shit out of me. Not in a bleeding-colon way, but close. In my mind, strip clubs were linked to bathhouses and leather bars and all the other things that meant AIDS in the late eighties and early nineties.

All I knew about D.C.'s gay strip clubs was what I had read. They were notorious nationwide because they allowed strippers to dance completely naked. (In most of the country, strippers have to cover up something—nipples, genitals, booty cracks—but in the nation's capital you could let it all hang, poke, or protrude out.) As one gay travel guide relayed:

> Perch on a bar stool, select a dancer (you'll find a nice variety, from long-haired blond boys to muscular military studs), produce a bill, and express your approval by rubbing it against his strong young ankle. He will respond by squatting before you. Slide your palm across his smooth, hard muscles—slip your hands between his thighs and finger that tight, butch butthole—grab the meat hanging in front of you, and milk it (no mouth action).

This quirk of the nation's capital made a lot of guys particularly proud to be American.

But I didn't know any of this as I made plans to see my porn star prince do his thing at La Cage. All I knew about stripping came from watching Gregory Harrison in *For Ladies Only* and Christopher Atkins in *A Night in Heaven*.

To ease my anxiety, I enlisted a good friend of mine to go with me. He was a tall, skinny Jewish guy named Seth, and he was probably one of the guys I'd be having sex with if I was actually having sex. I didn't know Seth well, but I liked what I knew. We had similar tastes—sushi, *alu paratha*, James Baldwin, Virginia Woolf. And our CD and cassette collections had a lot of overlap: MC Lyte's *Eyes on This*, Janet Jackson's *Rhythm Nation: 1814*, Madonna's first album, the Pet Shop Boys' *Actually*, Ten City's *Foundation*, and the debut by a new singer named Mariah Carey.

"Mariah's got a good voice, but the album's a little overproduced," Seth said one day when I was hanging out at his apartment listening to Public Enemy's "Welcome to the Terrordome."

But even more than the shared tastes in food, authors, and music, I liked Seth because I felt comfortable around him. I didn't have to act a certain way to get him to like me. Whenever he saw me, whether I was dressed to go out or unshaven and droopy-eyed after an all-nighter, his eyes always opened a little wider and his lips looked ready to smile.

I also appreciated that he agreed to go with me to the strip club to see Joey. A lot of people would've thought it was too kinky or weird. But Seth had my back, and he didn't judge me for wanting to go.

We headed to the club on a Friday night, and on the way there I got the strangest flashback feeling. We were driving on streets that, as a D.C. native, I'd traveled many times on the way to my grandmother's house (she lived about ten minutes away) and to my mother's job at one of the big federal office buildings. As a teenager, I'd sometimes see the glowing La Cage sign while in the car with my mother. I didn't know what the club was then, but it sure looked intriguing.

La Cage sat just blocks away from such national landmarks as the U.S. Capitol, the Washington Monument, and the White House. But the neighborhood was far from tourist friendly, full of abandoned buildings, vacant lots, and houses that looked like they were one brick away from being condemned. The block came alive only at night, when La Cage and the other clubs turned on their neon signs and all sorts of men looking to get it on with other guys descended upon the sidewalkless streets.

Seth and I arrived at La Cage, found a place to park, and tentatively stepped inside the side door entrance. We paid $5 each to a serious-looking man sitting in a booth and moved into the club's dark innards. There were two bars in the club, and standing on top of them were some of the hottest guys I'd ever seen, dancing completely naked save for their socks. The dancers were bathed in warm red light shining from above the bars. They glowed like dreams, and I was enthralled.

As I walked through the club, my eyes focused on this one particular dancer, a tall, athletic guy who looked like he could've modeled some polo shirts for Ralph Lauren. Watching him move across the bar reminded me of that scene from *Risky Business* where Tom Cruise dances around the living room in his underwear. I loved seeing such a private moment on the big screen, and I felt similarly about looking at Polo Guy.

It was great just to be able to gaze at a guy, naked or otherwise, and really be able to check him out. This was something I hadn't been able to do without fear since the second grade, when an incident happened at the home of my best friend, Teddy, a blond kid who was about a year younger than me. I went over his house to play almost every day after school, and I was perpetually fascinated because I'd never spent so much time in a white person's house. Every detail struck me as both familiar and strange, like watching *The Brady Bunch* in 3D and Smell-O-Vision.

We were in his bedroom going through our daily routine. He would ask me to turn around so that he could change from his school outfit into his play clothes, and every day I would comply. But on this particular day, something felt different. I wanted to look. I had to. It was like I'd lost the choice not to look. Slowly I peeked my head around, and caught a flash of blond hair, pale skin, and Superman Underoos. Then I saw Teddy's eyes as he looked up. Suddenly he lunged at me, pounding his small fists at my chest and screaming, "I told you to turn around. I told you not to look." I tried to get him off me as his mother—every white mom you've ever seen in a sitcom—came racing into the room.

"What on earth is going on here?" she asked, pulling her son toward her.

"Craig looked at me while I was changing," he yelled.

"What?"

"Craig looked at me while I was changing. I told him to turn around and he didn't."

Her eyes darted toward me. I felt my face burn red and tears start to well up in my eyes. I didn't know what to say.

"I think you should go home now," she told me. "Teddy's very upset."

"OK," I said, backing out of the room. "I'm sorry."

"It's fine. Just please go," she said, looking at me, not like I had done something bad but like I *was* something bad.

The next day my mother asked me why I wasn't going over to Teddy's house and I just told her that he got mad at me about something and that I didn't think we were friends anymore. Thankfully, she didn't press the issue. How could I admit that I lost my best friend because I couldn't help myself from wanting to see him naked? I didn't understand it myself, so how could I have explained it to my mom?

By the time I came out, some fifteen years later, I had at least owned up to the fact that I wanted to look at guys, but that didn't make it any easier to do. I never knew when I might look too long or too desirously and get my ass kicked—or worse. But here at the strip club, it was safe to look, and that made me feel powerful.

After Polo Guy finished his set, the D.J. announced that Joey would be coming on next. I grabbed Seth's hand and we moved through the crush of older guys and got right next to the bar. My heart pounded and my dick got hard. There was silence for a moment, then a song came over the speakers. No beat, just a hearty gospel voice over dreamy synthesizers: "Everybody, everybody . . . Everybody, everybody."

The crowd roared and all eyes turned to the left side of the bar, where Joey, his brown hair flopping over his forehead, stepped on the bar in jean shorts, an orange reflective vest, and a yellow construction hat. He seemed to move in slow motion, easing along the bar and waving his arms to the song's chant. He took off his clothes without any striptease pretense or fanfare. The crowd pushed closer to the bar. Joey dropped to his knees and lay down, arching his back and writhing to the music. Hands rushed toward him in every direction. Guys rubbed him all over, along his chest, on his cock, back and forth down his legs.

I was dying to touch him, but I was scared. I wasn't sure what the limits were. What if mine was the one hand that pushed him over the edge? He'd storm off and it'd be all my fault. I couldn't risk it. Could I?

But then I thought, this might be the one and only chance I'd ever have to lay hands on a guy who'd meant so much to my budding sense of gay-boy-ness. I was going over this in my head when a bulky unshaven guy behind me barked, "Look, if you're not gonna touch, move out of the way."

"What the hell," I thought as I stuck my hand out and reached toward Joey's balls, gingerly cupping them. My eyes quickly went to his face. It didn't register disgust so far as I could tell. He was still arching his back and writhing as a sea of hands washed over him. He stayed like this for a few minutes and my hand didn't leave his balls once. As I touched him, I realized that this was the first guy I'd ever felt in a sexual way. Unlike my straight friends and, say, all the teens I'd seen in movies and on TV, I'd never experienced drunken gropes on a basement couch, hands down pants in the back of a car, or stolen kisses behind the football field bleachers. This was it for me, the first naked guy I'd ever laid my hands on. When the song was over, Joey put on his clothes, thanked the crowd, and left the bar. I put my hand to my nose and swore it smelled like cherries.

3

I believe in the power of love . . . I believe in the power of love." The words thumped from the loudspeakers at Tracks, one of D.C.'s hottest gay nightclubs. It was a few days after the Joey Stefano show. Seth had called me and asked if I'd go dancing with him. I figured I owed him one so I said yes.

"Are you sure?" he asked, probably sensing my hesitation.

"Yeah," I said. "Sure. I'd really like to go."

"OK, I'll pick you up in about an hour."

"Cool."

I felt bad that I'd given him the impression that I didn't want to go. I did like him. The problem was that I didn't know *how* to like someone. What should I do? Carry a sign? Send up smoke signals? Maybe I should make him a mixtape?

About an hour later, Seth picked me up in his roommate's car and we headed to Tracks. The whole place was a sprawl of bars, large open spaces to dance, swirling lights, and dark corners. Most of the guys were young, flashy, and hot. But when I looked at them, trying to make eye contact, they either rolled their eyes and abruptly turned away or shot me a look like they wanted to devour me right then and there.

"You seem uptight," Seth said after we'd been standing around watching flocks of guys pass by. "Let's go dance."

"OK," I said, following him to the dance floor, where an extended mix of Deee-Lite's "Power of Love" was sending folks into a hands-in-the-air frenzy. After "Power of Love" faded into something else, we collapsed on a sofa near the dance floor.

"I really like that song," I said, smiling.

"Yeah, me too," Seth added. Then he put his right arm around me and I let him keep it there. For the first time in my life I let another guy hold me.

The next day, Seth called me at around four in the afternoon. I was still in bed.

"Hello," I answered groggily.

"Hey," he paused. "Did I wake you?"

"Sorta."

"Sorry. I just wanted to tell you that I bought that song you liked at the club, so if you want to come over . . ."

"You mean 'Power of Love'?"

"Yeah, the one we were dancing to last—"

"Oh, I already bought it."

"What? When? I thought you were still 'sleep."

"I really wanted it, so I stayed up until the record store opened at ten. Then I bought it, came home and played it, and went to sleep."

"You stayed up all night for it? That's insane."

"Yeah, well, I really wanted it. I'm just kinda like that about things."

"I see. Well, do you want to come over anyway and see if my CD sounds any different than yours?"

I didn't respond. Was this what it sounded like when someone was asking to have sex with you? I thought it might be. And I wasn't against having sex. I wanted it. It was about time.

"Uh, why don't you come over here? I mean, if you want."

"Cool. I'll be there after work."

That night, we had sex for the first time, following Seth's "You seem tense. Would you like a massage?" setup. Two weeks later, he moved into my one-room apartment.

Fast forward a couple of years, and we were still dating and happily living together. We'd finished college and had both decided to enter graduate programs at the University of Maryland—Seth in comparative literature, me in American studies. I felt like I was really becoming a grown-up, with my long-term relationship and my new career path to become an academic. Things were changing fast.

The one constant in all of this was that I continued to go to La Cage a couple of times a month, and even ventured out to the neighboring strip clubs Secrets and Wet.

"I just like them," I tried to explain to Seth once, while putting on my coat to go. "I like the atmosphere. It's fun and relaxing after a long week at school."

"Whatever makes you happy," he said from the bed, before returning to his book.

The truth was that I was happy about all the good things in my life like Seth and school, but I also felt that things were getting a little safe and predictable. The strip clubs excited me and gave me something to look forward to.

"Are you sure you don't mind if I go out?" I said from the door.

"No, I don't mind," he answered, not looking up from his book.

A couple of months later, I came up with the perfect reason for continuing to go to the clubs. I needed a topic for my master's thesis, something that I could study in an in-depth way for an extended period of time, and I immediately thought of writing about the strip clubs.

"So, I have this idea for my thesis," I said to my adviser, Dr. Sheri Parks, the only black professor in my department.

"OK," she said from behind the desk in her office.

"Well, it's a little offbeat and it has to do with gay culture and stuff."

"So, what is it?"

"Well, I was thinking of doing something about these gay strip clubs in D.C. They've been around for a while. They're sort of like local institutions. And I figured that maybe I could interview the strippers about why they work there and the customers about why they go and stuff like that."

She thought about it for a moment.

"It's racy but it sounds like a good idea. It will certainly make your work stand out," she said enthusiastically. "Go for it."

I was thrilled. I started going out a couple of times a week in the name of research. I came armed with a notebook, a tape recorder, and a wad of dollar bills for tips. My goal was to get at why the dancers decided to strip and how they felt about their work. My methodology was ethnography, which involved both interviewing and what's called participant observation, the process of studying something that you're also a part of. This particularly suited my needs, since I was already somewhat of a regular at the clubs. I couldn't suddenly pretend I was Jacques Cousteau snorkeling by a new species of fish.

The first person I asked to interview was a La Cage dancer named Jake, a tall, chiseled brunette whom everyone called "the Guess Model." I approached Jake first because he was one of the most popular dancers, and I figured I might as well go for broke. I don't remember exactly how I asked him. All I know is that after about a minute of stammering, sweating, and heart palpitations, I heard him say, "Yes."

"Really, you'll talk to me," I yelled giddily as 2 In A Room's acid-laced hip-house anthem "Wiggle It" blared in the background: "Wiggle it just a little bit / I wanna see you wiggle it just a little bit / as it grooves!"

"Sure," he said, naked, from atop the bar, his dangling dong about an inch from my nose. "Just wait until my set is over and we'll talk."

As I waited for Jake to get off the bar, I watched another dancer—a young redhead—who was bent over with his ass spread inches away from a customer's face. The customer, an older man with glasses and a comb-over, took his fingers and gently rubbed them between the dancer's butt cheeks. Then, when the dancer moved away, the man put his fingers to his nose, breathed deeply, and smiled. It still amazed me to see stuff like this play out in public.

Shortly thereafter, Jake finished his set and walked into the dressing room. My mind raced, wondering if there was a trapdoor back there or something. He'd disappear; I wouldn't get my interview; and I'd never graduate from the master's program. But just before I completely descended down my mental spiral of doom, he reemerged shirtless in a pair of jeans. To me, he looked a bit like John Travolta in *Saturday Night Fever*, if Travolta's character, Tony Manero, had spent as much time in a tanning bed as he did on the dance floor.

We began talking and Jake told me the story of how he got started. He used to work at a construction site where he was always teased for being a pretty boy. Finally he decided to make the pretty boy thing work for him. A friend brought him to La Cage, and Jake soon started making upward of $300 a night. He cut back on his construction work and now spent most days sleeping in while his buddies were toiling in the sun. He sometimes couldn't believe how much money he made just for standing around naked and letting old guys get touchy-feely.

"One night I was about to call in sick," he told me, "but I came in anyway and walked out with six hundred dollars."

"So I guess it was worth coming in?"

"Hell yeah."

There were so many questions that I had for him, all of which were written in a steno notepad I carried with me.

"How do you decide how long to stay with each customer?" I asked.

"Say if he's a regular and I know him really well, I'll sit there and talk to him for a few minutes. But if I don't know him, I'll just squat down for a short time and then pat him on his back and say, 'I've got to go, buddy.' The goal is to get him to tip again. That's called 'workin' them.' I've had guys give up twenty dollars in dollar bills. I've had guys give me fifties. This one guy, he gave me two hundred-dollar bills just for dancing."

"Wow," I responded. "So, hey, do you mind if I ask you a sort of personal question?"

"Shoot."

"If a customer asks if you're straight or gay, what do you tell him?"

"Bi. I mean, I'm straight. But I'll say I'm bi because the customers like to think there's a chance. And in a way I am bi because there's no way I could get up on the bar like that and let hundreds of men touch me if I wasn't. I mean, it's a sexual act because people are stroking me. It's not oral or anal, but still it's sexual. So, basically, I guess I'm bisexual, although I've never done it with a guy and don't think I would."

This was my introduction to how complex the idea of sexual identity could be at the clubs.

I interviewed Jake off and on for a couple of weeks and he introduced me to some of his coworkers, including a black dancer named Nico, who I also asked for an interview. To describe Nico, let's say you'd take Blair Underwood's head and transplant it on an NFL linebacker's body.

"I want to ask you some questions before I agree to this interview," Nico said as we sat at a table in the corner of the bar.

"Don't worry," I responded. "I'm not using real names or anything."

"Now that wasn't even what I was going to ask you. Do you put words in the mouth of everybody you interview?"

"Sorry."

He rolled his eyes in a way that immediately told me he was gay.

"What I was going to say is, do the people at your school already know what you're doing for your project?"

"Yeah. It's cool."

"Do they know you're gay?"

"How do *you* know I'm gay?"

"Oh, please. You spend more time here than the roaches, and that can't all be for school."

"OK, fine. I'm gay."

"And your school doesn't mind you writing about gay stuff?"

"Nope. Not yet at least."

"All right. I just don't want you to get in any trouble."

"Don't worry. I can handle myself."

He rolled his eyes again.

Nico got started after one of the managers spotted him at a nightclub dancing with his shirt off. "Well, I'm a dancer first and foremost, and when I go out to regular nightclubs, I always dance with my shirt off anyway. And when spandex was popular, I was always dancing in spandex, and that's just one step away from being naked."

He enjoyed it for a while—the freedom, the quick dough. But before long Nico was frustrated by the job because the other dancers, or as he put it, "any ol' scraggly white boy," pulled in more tips than he did.

"Even that little dirty motherfucker who wears those dingy, dirty, disgusting socks is making more than me," Nico griped, arching a finger toward another dancer. "He hasn't washed those socks for weeks. Then he goes sliding along the bar in those putrid things. Oh my God! Those socks are gray. The lights hit them and—oh, they are disgusting."

"Why do you think that is?"

"You're asking me why that dirty motherfucker doesn't wash his socks?"

"No," I said, shaking my head. "Why do you think he's making more money?"

"Well, obviously I have this deep tan here," he said,

pointing to his arm, the color of a Hershey bar. "And I feel that's the reason why they make more money. I'm not what most of the clientele is looking for.

"Watch me on my next set," he continued. "All of the other dancers can go around the bar and they might get a tip from a person who won't even acknowledge me, won't even look up. I mean, it's fucked up when someone ignores you like that. It hurts. It's almost like they're telling you, 'You don't look good enough to be naked,' and I'm not havin' it.

"Sometimes," he went on, "when I'm on the bar, people pull their money closer. There was this one white drag queen who came in here and pulled her purse closer to her. I'm like, 'What, am I gonna run, take your money or your bag, run back in the dressing room, get dressed, and then run out the door? What is a naked man gonna steal from you, huh?'"

"There must be some customers who like black guys."

"Well, either they want them real light-skinned like you or you get the ones who call themselves living dangerously and they're looking for a real roughneck. But unbeknownst to them, I'm not a roughneck. I don't want my nipples twisted and bitten and pinched and all that freaky shit. I like to be gentle like everybody else. I may look like a roughneck, but I'm not one, and I'm not trying to become one."

"Why do you keep working here if it's so bad?"

"Well, I really don't like this job. But the money is still good. You get forty dollars base pay just for showing up, and you can't beat the schedule. If I go out of town tomorrow and don't come back for the next year, I don't have to tell them anything. And then, when I get back, I just dance. No big deal."

I glanced at the questions on my steno pad.

"You know what I've always wanted to know? When you're out there and the customers are jerking you off, how do you keep from cumming?"

"Usually," he deadpanned, "you just look at one of them."

4

One night I was at La Cage struggling to make my watery glass of Coke last so that I wouldn't have to put out $5 for another one. It got expensive going to clubs all the time on a grad student stipend, and it would be hard to explain to Seth that we could eat only ramen for the next month because I'd spent all of our money on tips and overpriced drinks.

The bar wasn't very crowded. There were plenty of empty stools, so I was a little surprised when a guy came over and sat right next to me. I recognized him immediately. He was another regular, routinely making the rounds of all the local strip clubs. I'd noticed him before because he was a sort of rock star among the customers, frequently surrounded by the cutest dancers at the bar or sometimes tucked in a shadowy corner with just one dancer. They'd be sitting closely together, exchanging hushed words, their faces nearly touching.

His popularity was a bit odd because he wasn't the coolest-looking guy in the world. He was probably in his late fifties, yet he had the gawky gait of a teenager after his first major growth spurt. His face was a small round bulb punctuated by wide eyes and a protruding nose, capped by a gray Romanesque crown of hair.

"Do you mind if I sit here?" he asked.

I gave him a "free country" shrug of the shoulders and went back to carefully tensing my cheek muscles so that I was taking the smallest possible sips of Coke.

"Listen," he continued, "I don't want to intrude on your personal space, but if you want somebody to talk to, you're welcome to join me."

I found this strange, since he had already taken the stool to my right. Wasn't he technically joining *me*?

"But," he said, "if you prefer to be alone, that's fine, too."

Thanks for telling me it's OK to be as I was, I thought. After all this time going to strip clubs by myself, I had developed a kind of protective coating when it came to the advances of other customers. I knew all the lines, which basically amounted to numerous drunken variations on "Are you a dancer? You should be." It wasn't that I minded some casual bar flirting, but I found that if I started talking to these guys, either they wouldn't leave me alone or they would do something else to make me regret ever opening the conversational portal.

One time, I was talking to this cute guy in his late thirties about work, his dogs, and the movies we both liked, when all of a sudden he stopped midthought and said, "Wait a minute. You're not a hustler, are you? Because I'm not going to pay to have sex with you."

These kinds of experiences made me reluctant to talk to other customers. But since I had seen this guy around a lot *and* I was trying to make my Coke last, I said, "I'm Craig. What's your name?"

"Dave," he answered, shaking my hand. "I've seen you here and at the other clubs."

"Yeah." I nodded. "You seem to get around, too."

The bartender, a brown-haired guy in a sleeveless muscle shirt, passed by and took Dave's drink order, a gin and tonic. Then he disapprovingly eyed my drink, which was about three-fourths empty and had taken on the color of drain ditch water.

"You want another one of those?" the bartender asked.

"Uh . . . sure," I said, and I could almost feel my pockets getting lighter.

"You can put that on my tab," Dave said.

"Thanks. That's really nice."

"You're welcome."

"So what brings you out tonight, other than the obvious?" I said, gesturing toward a dancer walking our way.

"Well, I usually come out on Friday and Saturday nights. It's my reward for being good all week."

"What do you do?"

"I work for the federal government. I'm in management," he answered as the bartender returned with our drinks.

"Have you been coming out to the clubs for long?"

"Well, I used to be married. I was married for twenty-one years. But after the divorce . . . many years after the divorce, I started coming out. First, I went to the clubs in Baltimore. I was a little concerned about running into people I knew from the office or maybe even my ex-wife. But one day I got tired of making the thirty-minute drive."

"So, you obviously enjoyed yourself once you started coming here?"

"I was like a kid in a candy store. I hadn't touched a man in twenty-one years because I was in a monogamous straight relationship. After all that time having these desires and then all of a sudden it's available—I kind of went bonkers." He took a sip from his drink and then asked, "What about you?"

"Well, I'm actually here for school," I started, but I noticed his attention had drifted away. He was staring at a dancer who had just climbed onto the bar. I'd met the dancer before. His name was Matt. He was a nice guy but not my type at all. He had dark hair; he was older, probably in his late twenties; and unlike his shaved and naturally smooth coworkers, Matt sported a thin coat of shiny black hair over his tall, gym-hardened frame.

On this night, he was a vision of seeming contradictions, with thick, black-rimmed glasses, neatly combed hair, and black leather chaps that exposed both his butt and his dangling dick. He also held a leather riding crop in his hand, which made him come off like a naughty

33

librarian who dished out kinky penalties for overdue books.

Matt looked at Dave and then he snapped his fingers, motioning for Dave to come over.

"Excuse me a moment," Dave said, getting up from his stool and walking toward where Matt was standing. There were people seated in front of Matt, but they had to scoot over to make room for Dave. As soon as Dave was in front of him, Matt kneeled down. Dave put a buck in one of Matt's socks and took a round mini tub of Elbow Grease from the other. He liberally applied the lube to Matt's dick and started working on it for several minutes, stretching and pulling, until it stood fully erect. The customers, who'd been pushed to the side, were now watching intently.

Once Dave helped li'l Matt reach his full growth potential, the other customers started to clap. "Thank you," Matt said to Dave as he stood up and stepped over toward his other admirers. Dave, all smiles, headed back my way. He sat down, grabbed a couple of cocktail napkins off the bar, and wiped his hands.

"That was fun," he said. "No matter where I am, Matt will pick me out and I have to go service him. Even if there are people lined up three and four deep at the bar, they have to clear a place for me. Matt will stand there until I take care of him because the hard-ons help him make money." Dave grinned proudly and continued, "Matt says that I should teach masturbation at the college level.

"He's a nice kid, but typical Generation X. He can't figure out what to do with himself," Dave said, taking another sip of gin and tonic. "So, what were you saying about school? I'm the type of person who can start a conversation, walk away, and then pick it up ten years later without missing a beat."

"Oh, I was just saying that I'm sorta here for school. I'm in grad school and I'm studying the clubs for my master's thesis."

"Really?"

"I know it sounds weird."

"The people at your school allow you to do that?"

"Yeah, it's all about understanding sexual subcultures, yadda yadda yadda. I'm interviewing a bunch of dancers about why they strip."

"What do they say?"

"Well, it's complicated. But most of them say they just do it for money."

"Yep, I've heard that, too. But let's face it, there are a lot of other ways to make money. You can do construction, hang drywall, or whatever. You don't have to take off your clothes for money and let guys play around with you."

"Yeah, I guess."

One of the things I'd noticed since starting my research is that so many people, even those who'd never stepped foot in a strip club, felt they knew exactly why people chose to strip, and these homegrown theories almost always contradicted what the strippers themselves had to say.

Dave said, "Now one of the things I've heard is, 'Where can I make this much money in so few hours and at the same time have people buy me drinks and I can drink on the job?'"

"You don't believe that?"

"I think money is part of it. But some of these guys are really narcissistic, really into themselves. So I think that exhibitionism is another big factor. But the really big reason is that a lot of these guys just need attention. A lot of them are starved for love and affection. Many I've talked to come from broken homes and they want that approval from you in the worst way."

"What makes you think that?"

"Well, an example is the way they'll come over and flex their muscles for you. It's like a little kid showing off for Daddy. I think I'm a father figure to some of them. There's this one guy, a cute kid, whose father was an abusive alcoholic who was in the military. It sounded like the dad probably beat him a lot. And here I am, this older guy who will listen to him and not be judgmental. You can tell it strikes a chord with him."

"And what do *you* get out of it?"

"I sometimes explain it to my other gay friends like this. Going to a regular gay bar is a lot like fishing. You have to spend four or five hours hoping that you're gonna get one fish that wants your hook. But by coming here, I can eliminate all of that. I know that there will be some hot young guys and I can stroke them. And stroking dicks is probably my favorite form of sex. I love doing it. There's nothing more satisfying to me than playing with another guy's dick. I really get a kick out of making another guy feel good. So by coming to the clubs, I'm guaranteed to be able to get what I'm looking for, and I can do it within a very narrow time frame."

"So, it's efficient?"

"Exactly."

5

After my first talk with Dave, I started running into him nearly every week. We'd sit next to each other and share observations on our favorite dancers. Dave was partial to Peter, a cherubic twenty-one-year-old former wrestler prone to earnestly spewing archaic phrases like "Thank you kindly" and "Much appreciated" every time he was tipped.

"He's such a sweet kid," Dave once said. "I love him to death. I still like that eighteen-to-twenty-four-year-old look, like a teenager just starting to become a man. That's where I'm sexually frozen in time."

As we got to know each other better, Dave slowly revealed to me how he'd gone from being this seemingly straight guy who was married for more than two decades to becoming a gay strip club regular. His story was just another example of how, the longer I hung out at the clubs, the more complicated I thought the whole idea of sexuality was. It was easy to think of the customers as just dirty old men, but many, like Dave, had led lives that had been full of secrets and compromise. That made their time at the clubs seem less like a hedonistic indulgence and more like a taste of hard-won freedom.

Dave first figured out he was attracted to other guys while growing up on a Louisiana farm in the 1940s. At age nine, he developed a crush on an older cousin. "He was such a hot-looking, well-built guy, and when it came to sports, you name it, and he did it—boxing, football, wrestling, every-thing," Dave told me. "He was everything I wasn't but wanted to be."

Sometimes this cousin, an endearing show-off, would jerk off around Dave, but Dave never joined in, which he still regrets. "Now I kick myself because he was one gor-geous guy," Dave said. "But I was going to Catholic school at the time, and I had a lot of moral dilemmas in terms of religion."

Instead, Dave found other outlets for his desires. One day he went to Montgomery Ward to buy a Bike jock strap because his cousin always wore one. As he held it in the store, he could barely contain his excitement. "I was so aroused," he said, "I was surprised I didn't cum in my shorts."

He took the jock strap home and stashed it in a seldom-used drawer. It was like a talisman of sexual energy. Some-times he wore it outside the house just for a thrill. "When I went to a school dance or something, I would put it on because guys used to talk about how they needed to wear jock straps so they wouldn't get hard-ons," he recalled.

"Well, dancing with girls normally didn't make me pop a boner, but I wore that jock strap just the same. To this day, jock straps make me aroused."

Wearing the jock strap also made him more comfortable with his burgeoning sexuality. Where he once feared that playing with himself would put him on the fast track to hell, his new motto became "God gave it to you; it's for you to use." He and some other cousins who lived nearby started retreating to various corners of the family farm, masturbating and helping one another get off. "We all jerked off together from the time we were, maybe, eleven or twelve," Dave remembered.

A couple of years later, Dave was shopping in the city closest to his farm. He was flipping through some comic books at the City Newsstand when his eyes came upon a handful of digests featuring cover images of shiny, oiled young men flexing their muscles and wearing little more than jock strap–like bits of cloth. He bought one of the magazines and brought it home, hiding it in the drawer next to his jock strap. Although the magazine said it was dedicated to health, fitness, and the well-developed male physique, Dave said that he "always had a feeling that they were appealing to somebody who likes guys."

Dave would flip through the magazines imagining himself with the models in the pictures. He would also try to see if he could catch any glimpses of the private parts that the posing straps were trying to hide. "I remember once I could see the head of a guy's penis," he said. "The picture was very dark, but, man, did I jerk off to that thing."

Despite his strong feelings, Dave didn't think he had the option of acting on them. This was in the early fifties, when homosexuality was considered a mental illness and acting on it was a crime. "I just didn't see how I could be a part of that lifestyle," Dave said.

Dave fooled around with one guy in college, but after that he focused exclusively on women, concerning himself more with their pleasure than his own. "I always wanted to make a woman cum," he explained, "and if she couldn't reach an orgasm, I mean, that was just totally frustrating to me because I wanted to please her."

To satisfy his own urges, Dave headed to movie theaters that showed nudist films. "These movies were always taken at nudist camps," Dave remembered, "and a lot of them centered around the volleyball court. I guess that gave them an excuse to show a lot of big boobs bouncing up and down. Unfortunately, they generally didn't have men frontal. They let you see the butts, but that was about it. I'd be thinking, 'Please, please, please let me see some pubic hair.'"

By this time, the mid-sixties, Dave was living in D.C. doing classified work for the military. He was on his own and away from Louisiana, but still no more able to act on his desires. "You could not be gay doing the work that I was doing," he told me. "I had top secret clearance. It was very likely that I was tailed on a regular basis. So during that whole period, there's no way I could have been gay. I would have been court-martialed."

Because of this, Dave continued dating women, and at

thirty-one, he met the one who would become his wife. "Things started clicking," he remembered, "and the next thing you know, I'm getting married." Still, he had doubts about whether or not it was the right thing to do, given his feelings for men. "There was always this gnawing fear that I was gay and it was not going to work," he said. "But I just decided that this was a commitment I was making, and I realized that my life was not going to be perfect in the sense that there was always going to be something unfulfilled. But then I thought most people's lives are unfulfilled to some degree. It's just something you live with."

Dave married in 1970 and although he never cheated on his wife, he did find ways to satisfy his desires for men. Dave and his wife regularly took trips to Broadway to see the latest productions, and late at night, Dave would head out by himself to check out the live sex shows in Times Square. "The performers were usually young Puerto Ricans, a guy and a girl," he recalled. "I'd go and watch them screw their heads off. But I was really watching the guy. I didn't give a shit about the girl. The guys were usually hung like horses, and they'd be turning me on. So I always found little outlets for myself that didn't involve actual contact with another guy."

Dave's other outlet was going to X-rated movie houses. He even told his wife about his penchant for porn and she said that it didn't bother her. He developed a routine: On Monday evenings after he ate dinner with his wife and helped with the dishes, he'd jump in the car and go to one of the many porn theaters that used to light up downtown D.C. He'd go only to the ones showing straight films, because he was scared to be spotted going to a gay movie house. He even avoided the theaters that showed both straight and gay films.

On those nights when it took him longer than usual to leave, his wife would sometimes ask, "Aren't you going to the movies?"

"Are you sure you don't mind?"

"No, go ahead," she'd say.

After parking and before going in the theater, Dave would pop his trunk and take out a nylon windbreaker that he always kept in there. He'd then go in the theater, find a seat away from everyone else, and spread his thin jacket over his lap. He'd watch the straight couples having sex on the screen and jerk off for as long as he could without cumming. It was his reward for being a good husband throughout the week. "That was the way I compensated," he said.

This was how he passed the years as the seventies turned into the eighties. But his whole life changed one night in 1989 when his wife said that she was leaving him to be with another man. The marriage that he'd sacrificed his sexual desires for was over.

This was just the first tumbling rock of what would become an avalanche of problems. His mother, who'd been living alone in Louisiana since his father passed, took a fall and wound up bedridden, requiring round-the-clock care. Some real estate he'd inherited took a 90 percent dip in value, and at work Dave lost a promotion to a close friend. Compounding this, a trip to the doctor revealed that his pancreas was malfunctioning, a particularly disturbing development since his father died of pancreatic cancer.

Dave remembered this as the lowest point in his life. "I started going through some pretty bad depression," he said. "I was having a lot of suicidal thoughts. It was a really bad period and as a result I just totally reexamined my life and made a lot of changes. I came to the conclusion that as much as possible, I would try to enjoy every single day."

By the time I met Dave, he was divorced and had been coming to the strip clubs for several years. "I'm closeted almost everywhere else," he said, quickly adding, "I hope."

"Do you ever think about totally coming out?" I asked him one night over another watery Coke.

"If I were younger, I think I probably would come out. There are times when I'm really tempted to come out, at least with some friends. I've always been a very open person about my life and it's difficult to keep part of it hidden. But then I think it would be uncomfortable, especially with guys at work that I've been friends with for twenty years. All of a sudden, they're going to feel uncomfortable going into the bathroom and taking a leak beside me. I think, 'Why go through that?'"

"Have you told your ex-wife you're gay?"

"No. I know it's kind of ridiculous because she was the one who left me. But I always kind of felt like if she knew I was into the gay scene, it would invalidate the twenty-one years that we were together."

"Are you happier now?" I asked.

But before he could answer, Peter came over and knelt in front of us. Dave put a folded wad of dollars into Peter's white sport sock, and then took some lube from the other sock and dabbed it on Peter's slowly growing cock.

"Much appreciated," Peter said.

6

On a chilly morning in early February, Seth dropped me off on the corner of Ninth and G streets, NW, right outside the mammoth Martin Luther King Jr. Memorial Library downtown. I logged a lot of time there, studying up on the history of gay life in D.C. and how the strip clubs fit in. Seth, on the other hand, spent his days doing temp work at various offices around town. Although the two of us were in graduate school and receiving some financial aid, we couldn't afford for both of us not to work. So, since Seth was the one with typing skills, he was the one with the day job. (Metaphorically speaking, Seth brought home the bacon; I spent all day researching the history of pork products.) It didn't seem fair, and I sometimes felt uncomfortable about it. But I figured that in long-term relationships these sort of imbalances work themselves out.

"Learn something for me," Seth said, before giving me a hug and then heading off in our wildly unreliable and quite dinged-up Acura, a hand-me-down gift from my mother. He soon disappeared in the thick of morning traffic.

I went inside and strategically scoped out a desk that was in an aromatic safe zone, away from some of the more fragrant homeless people who liked to congregate at the library and spend all day thumbing through back issues of *Jet*. I pulled out my books and articles and got to work, trying to treat this as much like a job as I imagined Seth had to do with his temp assignments.

As I continued studying the clubs, I was learning that they were just another part of the surprisingly rich gay history of the city, which was designed with its unique four-part structure (NW, NE, SW, SE) by French-born Pierre L'Enfant, a man alternately described as "affected," "of artistic and fragile temperament," and "sensitive in style and dress"—all possible codes for "queer as fuck."

In the 1800s, when the nation was at war with itself, poet Walt Whitman, known for rhapsodizing about "We two boys together clinging / One the other never leaving," came to town to care for injured federal soldiers. He tended wounds and spoon-fed ice cream to the young enlisted men, many of whom were tasting it for the very first time. One evening in the city, a nearly fifty-year-old Walt met Irish immigrant Peter Doyle, who was more than twenty years his junior, on a horse carriage going from the Navy Yard to Georgetown. They fell for each other instantly. "I put my hand on his knee; we understood," Walt wrote.

Soon Walt was calling Peter "the youth who loves me and whom I love," and they were spending days walking the Capitol grounds and nights at the bar in Georgetown's Union Hotel, "content, happy in being together, speaking little, perhaps not a word."

Around the same time that Walt was in town, there were published accounts of black men and white men having sex in Lafayette Square, "under the shadows of the White House," according to one writer. There was another article from the 1800s that chronicled an annual "Negro" drag ball, an "orgie of lascivious debauchery," as one writer put it, which found its participants "dressed in womanly attire, short sleeves, low-necked dresses and the usual ball-room decorations and ornaments of women, feathered and rib-boned head-dresses, garters, frills, flowers, [and] ruffles." But by far the most eye-catching element of the evening was a guy who stood butt naked on a pedestal with his "phallic member . . . decorated by a ribbon." According to Dr. Charles Hughes, who wrote about this phenomenon for a medical journal, this cross-dressing bacchanal brought together "cooks, barbers, waiters and other employees of Washington families, some even higher in the social scale—some even being employed as subordinates in the Government departments."

As I read about this, I wondered if I would've been one of the "Negroes" at this party—or would I have been too scared to go, living a life of celibacy in the servants' quarters of some white family's house? I called Seth at work to get his opinion. I usually tried not to bother him at one of his temp jobs, but this question was pressing on me. I went to the library's bank of pay phones and placed a call.

"Hey, um, sorry to bother you. And this might seem a little off-the-wall. You're not in the middle of anything, are you?"

"I have to get some photocopying done for a meeting. But what's up?"

"Oh, nothing. I shouldn't bother you now."

"No, what is it? Is something wrong?"

"Well, no. Um, I'm just asking, hypothetically speaking, if I'd been living in the eighteen hundreds, do you think I would've had the nerve to either have sex with guys in Lafayette Square or go to a drag ball?"

There was a long pause. I could hear the buzz and hum of office machines in the background.

"Hello?" I asked.

"Yeah, I'm not sure I understand."

"See, I just read that in the late eighteen hundreds guys used to have sex in Lafayette Square, near the White House, and they'd also go to these drag balls where the centerpiece decoration was some guy with a ribbon around his"—I quickly scanned the phone booth area to make sure I wasn't talking too loudly—"cock. I just wondered if you thought I would've had the nerve to go to these things, or would I have been too scared to go?"

"I'm not sure. It sounds kind of risky for you."

"What do you mean? I go to the strip clubs all the time."

"Yeah, but you go to watch. These things sound like

something you have to *do*. Besides, going to a legitimate nightclub today is not the same as hooking up in the park or going to some kind of underground drag ball in the eighteen hundreds. But can we talk about this more later? I really have to get these copies done."

"OK," I said, deflated. My own boyfriend didn't think I had the hypothetical balls to have sex in the park or go to a drag ball in the eighteen hundreds. Was I that much of a wimp? I packed up my stuff and took a lunch break.

When I returned, still smarting over my lack of a nineteenth-century sex life, I decided to jump ahead to World War II, when thousands of gay men flocked to the city from small towns in order to serve their country or find what locals called "a good government job." They hung out at food joints like Johnnie's in Southeast, the Cozy Corner near Howard University, and the Chicken Hut on L Street. Years later, filmmaker John Waters described the Hut as filled with "gay men in fluffy sweaters who cruised each other by calling table-to-table on phones provided by the bar."

Hanging out in restaurants was all the rage then because, following Prohibition, Congress—which regulates all of D.C.'s laws—made it so that only restaurants were eligible for liquor licenses. Therefore, for several decades, every place serving cocktails in the nation's capital had to have a fully equipped kitchen on the premises.

But little of this bothered those Greatest Generation types who arrived in D.C. during the war and congregated in these spots after work and on weekends. For many of them, it was an emancipating dream, to freely connect for the very first time with other guys who liked guys.

This sense of freedom was short-lived, however, due to the Cold War paranoia of the 1950s. Gays, thought to be especially vulnerable to blackmail threats, were branded as security risks and banned from federal employment. Hundreds of gay men and women lost their good government jobs.

Frank Kameny was one of them. The product of a middle-class Jewish family from New York, Frank came to D.C. in the midfifties after earning a Ph.D. in astronomy from Harvard. He taught for a year at Georgetown and then landed a cushy civil service job with the U.S. Army Map Service. But after an arrest in Lafayette Park, the same cruising area that had been popular since the 1800s, he lost his job and was banned from future government employment. But instead of simply accepting this turn of fate, Kameny sued the government, picketed in front of the White House, and tried to take his case before the Supreme Court. The experience transformed him into an activist. He founded a local gay rights group in the 1960s that drew inspiration from the Black Power movement. Where Stokely Carmichael proclaimed, "Black is beautiful," Kameny led the call "Gay is good."

Kameny's slogan, while tame by today's standards, reflected the radicalism of the age. In 1968, a year that saw much of the U Street corridor—once the pride of black

D.C.—burn in the uprisings following Dr. Martin Luther King Jr.'s assassination, another, lesser-known protest took place at a gay club in southeast Washington called Plus One.

Plus One was the city's first gay-owned club to allow same-sex dancing, and because of this, it often attracted the attention of police officers, who would show up and try to scare away those standing in the long lines to get in the club. But on this particular evening, Kameny remembered, "The police pulled up and expected everyone to go run to the bushes and hide. But nobody moved, so they advanced down the street, and still nobody moved. They regrouped and got more cars and more police, and advanced down the street again, but still nobody moved. So the police just got in their cars and went home." This standoff took place one year before the riot at New York's Stonewall Inn, the event credited with birthing the modern lesbian and gay rights movement.

As the 1960s raged into the 1970s, politics increasingly went alongside the pursuit of pleasure. Gay men were no longer willing to keep their desires secret. The late sixties saw the Regency, located in the heart of downtown, become the city's first gay bathhouse; and in 1975, just blocks away, the city got its first gay strip club, the Chesapeake House.

The way this came about was rather haphazard. Owner John Rock planned the place to be a cozy piano bar, but one night on a whim he offered two sailors stationed in the area $50 to strip down and dance for his patrons. They took him up on the offer and suddenly this squat brick building, steps away from the National Portrait Gallery, became not only D.C.'s first gay strip club but one of the nation's first gay establishments to legally allow guys to bare all. Ironically, the city's otherwise restrictive liquor laws allowed fully nude dancing.

The 'Peake, as it was called by regulars, became nationally renowned, drawing a slew of visitors, including—according to local lore—Truman Capote, Tennessee Williams, and Rock Hudson. Over the years, the 'Peake developed a reputation for being a place where, as one customer put it, "older financiers met younger entrepreneurs." In 1980 it made national headlines when Maryland's conservative Republican congressman Robert Bauman, a married father of four and close friend of Ronald Reagan, was arrested for having sex with one of the club's dancers.

After the 'Peake success, other gay bars—like Dolly's and the Fraternity House—began featuring naked guys shaking and showing off their wares. But perhaps the gay strip club with the most interesting history, one that speaks to D.C.'s often peculiar pairing of sex and politics—red lights with red tape—was the Lone Star Steakhouse.

Opened as a Texas-style steak house in 1955, the Lone Star, which sat across the street from the FBI's mammoth, compoundlike headquarters, had transformed into a female go-go bar by the late 1970s, when it was seized by the U.S. Department of Justice because the owner was convicted of embezzlement. This left the task of running a nudie bar to a bunch of blue-suited bureaucrats, who in the interest of public stewardship had to ensure that the bar was profitable. This arrangement lasted for a couple of years, until increased public scrutiny forced the government to sell the club.

The new owner, a former elementary school teacher, decided that the best way to maximize his profits was to keep the nubile young women stripping during the day to cater to all the straight guys who commuted daily from the suburbs, but to add nude guys dancing at night to lure in the gay crowd. The Lone Star enjoyed a successful run until 1986.

In the 1980s, the gay strip club scene started becoming concentrated around O Street in southeast Washington. This area—part ghetto, part industrial wasteland—had become a safe haven for all different sorts of gay sexual establishments since the late 1970s. The businesses set up shop in this neighborhood—nearly forgotten by most Washingtonians even though it was only blocks from most of the major national landmarks—as a way to escape police harassment and public scrutiny.

"It became an out-of-sight, out-of-mind kind of thing," explained Kameny. "It was our piece of Washington."

For a time, the gay bars, movie houses, and bathhouses within this few-block radius were nearly devoid of public services. When it snowed, owners got together to plow the streets themselves; and for security, a group of gay ex-marines, calling themselves GEMS, joined together to patrol the streets with a German shepherd in tow. But conditions improved for the businesses when Marion Barry, a liberal black civil rights activist, became mayor in 1978 on the strength of a platform that, among other things, promised to put an end to raids on gay bars.

The area thrived. In 1984, O Street's first gay strip club, La Cage Aux Follies, opened, followed four years later by Secrets. These new clubs resided on the same block as the Follies, the gay movie house that already featured nude dancers on weekends. These three establishments together on the same block turned O Street into the city's gay strip club epicenter; and because D.C. still had one of the nation's most permissive policies regarding nudity, it became, by extension, the gay strip club capital of the country.

Yet what was ultimately most significant about the clubs was not their close proximity or the nudity itself; rather, the lack of government intrusion, due to Barry's mandate, allowed the clubs to develop their own set of rules about what was and wasn't permissible. It soon became par for the course that a stripper could play with his dick while dancing and that a customer could touch the dancer in any place the dancer allowed. This made for deeply intimate exchanges.

As I sat in the library reading about this history, I marveled at the way all these elements had to be put into play just so I could go out and see some hot guy show his prick. What seemed like a trivial flash of flesh was deeply connected to an array of social and cultural shifts, political gains and losses, personal acts of whimsy and courage, and a whole lot of grace and chance. I was itching to call Seth and tell him about all of this, but I figured I had already played my "Indulge Me" card for the day. So instead, I left the library early and went to the offices of the local gay newspaper, the *Washington Blade,* to place a Valentine's Day wish for my hardworking, very understanding guy. Using the title of one of our favorite Janet Jackson songs, the wish read: "To Seth . . . 'Because of Love.'"

7

In spring 1994, I finished the first draft of my master's thesis, which focused on how strippers and customers made sense of their experiences at the clubs. One of the things I tried to establish was the connection between what went on in the strip clubs and the things that were important within gay culture generally. I tried to explain how a guy's ass is revered within gay culture much the way a woman's breasts are treated like twin deities by straight guys. Or as I wrote in my most practiced academese: "Before discussing how the anus operates as a site of desire within the context of the clubs, . . . I think it is important to briefly problematize the relationship between the anus or anal sex and gay sex in general since they are often assumed to be one and the same."

To make my point, I cited examples of butt love from throughout gay culture. I quoted from the "Sonnet du Trou du Cul" (Sonnet on the Asshole) by those nineteenth-century fudgepacking French poets Paul Verlaine and Arthur Rimbaud: *"Obscur et froncé comme un œillet violet . . . Ma bouche s'accoupla souvent à sa ventouse"* (Crumpled like a carnation, mauve and dim . . . My mouth mates often with this breathing hole). I also referenced gay porn videos like *Butt Busters* and *Rear Window.*

But by far the most controversial thing I did in the thesis—though it seemed like a good idea at the time—was to include an appendix with photocopies of pictures from gay porn magazines featuring models doing a full bent-over ass-cheek spread. I thought the photos helped drive my argument home. However, when I met with one of my committee members—a bearded, bespectacled gentleman who was like the Platonic ideal of what a professor should be—he told me that the thesis, pics and all, had caused some problems for him when he in fact drove it home.

Apparently, he'd left it on his kitchen table one day. His wife was straightening up and stumbled upon it. She decided, perhaps, that it looked interesting, and browsed through it, becoming shocked, however, when she came across the booty gallery in the back. As the professor told me what happened, I imagined his stunned better half rapidly turning the pages and the butt cheeks flying by in moving succession like cartoon characters in a flip book.

"I'm soooo sorry," I said as I felt my whole body go hot and crimson.

"Oh, it's nothing, really," he responded with a wave of his hand. "Just a little awkward for a moment."

Still, I was never sure if he'd completely gotten over having Xerox copies of spread-eagled ass strewn across the same place where he took his morning muesli.

I graduated with my master's degree in May 1994 after turning in the final version of my thesis, "Desire and Dollar Bills: An Ethnography of a Gay Male Striptease Club in Washington, D.C." I had never felt such a sense of accomplishment, and my life seemed more complete than ever before. The thesis dedication read: "To Seth . . . for everything."

It was a great moment for both of us, since Seth graduated at the same time. Emboldened by the success, we both decided to go for our Ph.D.'s, which entailed new responsibilities. I taught my own class, "Introduction to American Studies," and I had to come up with a topic for my Ph.D. dissertation, which needed to be longer and more ambitious than my thesis. I knew I wanted to continue studying the clubs, but I didn't know how I could make my study sufficiently different from the thesis.

That is, until one day I was hanging out with Nico at the Follies (not to be confused with La Cage Aux Follies). Unlike the strip clubs, which operated at night, the Follies was a twenty-four-hour porn theater with a dark, maze-like backroom. It featured dancers on weekends with five shows a day: noon, 3:00 PM, 6:00 PM, 9:00 PM, and midnight. On Sundays, the theater served a free buffet-style dinner following the 6 PM show. The dancers would finish their set, quickly get dressed, and then race to a kitchen next door to grab big aluminum foil trays of food, usually of the beef Stroganoff or spaghetti and meatballs variety. Then the dancers would come back and set up the buffet for the customers.

On this particular day, I was sitting with Nico after he and the other dancers had just finished with the buffet. We were in the theater's electric blue *Miami Vice*–like lobby. *Dr. Quinn, Medicine Woman* played on the overhead TV.

"If you're so interested in stripping," Nico asked, "why don't you try it yourself?"

The question startled me. My mouth dried up and I didn't know what to say.

"I don't really think it's my thing."

"Your thing? So what is your thing, coming in here and asking everybody nosy-ass questions?"

"That's for school."

"Oh, please. You use that school excuse every time you don't want to own up to why you're really here all the time."

"OK, fine. I like hanging out here. I like looking at naked guys. Sue me."

"I think you want to try it but you're chickenshit."

A customer standing near the red gumball machines glanced over.

"I'm not chickenshit. I've just never thought about it."

"Now you've gone from chickenshit to bullshit."

"I just don't think it would be the right thing for me to do."

"Oh, so you think you're better than everybody else?"

"I didn't say that."

"You're so full of it. You say stripping is this cool thing

and that's why you want to write about it for school, but apparently it's not cool enough for someone like *you* to try."

"Maybe I will try it one day."

"Then that'll be the first day you've been real since you've been here," he said, and then turned his attention back to the frontier adventures of Jane Seymour.

I got up and walked toward the concession machines in front of the bathroom. Something about them always made me smile. I think it was the way the soda machine didn't say "Coke" or "Pepsi" but just "Cold Drinks." And the automated coffee machine was one of those pre-Starbucks contraptions that pissed brown fluid into a Dixie cup and offered options for "Extra Strong," "Extra Light," and "Extra Sugar."

I didn't know why I couldn't admit to anyone that I really did want to try stripping. The simple answer was just that I was scared. Scared about whether or not I could do it. Scared about what it would mean to do it. But I definitely didn't want the other dancers, many of whom I'd known for years now, to think that I felt I was better than they were.

The truth was that stripping had long called out to me. It offered something different from my grad school grind of dealing with students, grading papers, and sitting through seemingly endless seminars. It also felt like something I needed to do, a rite of passage of sorts. Since I'm too old to be a Gen-Xer, I've often thought of myself as Generation M, for Madonna. Throughout the eighties and nineties, the Material Girl made it acceptable to brazenly use your sexuality to get what you desired, to writhe around in your underwear on your way to the top. In fact, if you weren't able to use your looks and sexuality to get ahead, it was like you were the physical equivalent of dumb. My friends and I were constantly evaluating ourselves on our looks. "Am I hot or not?" was the new "Why was I born?"

But this issue of attractiveness went deeper for me. See, for as long as I could remember, as far back as elementary school, I've felt older guys watching me, hungrily—making eye contact as I walked through the mall holding hands with my grandmother, or gazing down as they stood beside me at a men's room urinal. These looks both frightened and fascinated me, and I grew to expect them in such a way that I became anxious both when I got the looks and when I didn't.

These feelings followed me into my teens. Sometimes when I caught an older guy staring at me, I'd wonder if I was doing something that was causing it, if I was sending a signal that I didn't know about. Once I went to the movies with my dad, who was then divorced from my mom. This was one of our few days together and I was pretty excited about it. We were running late so he stood in the popcorn line while I went to get seats. I walked in the theater and it was so dark I could barely see, but it wasn't very crowded. I grabbed two seats on the aisle toward the middle.

The previews started and I was watching intently when I felt someone sit down next to me. I assumed it was my dad but when I looked over, I saw it was an older white guy in a tweed coat and a hat. This freaked me out, but I wasn't sure what to do. The man next to me didn't say anything, but I could hear him breathing in long wheezes. Finally I saw my dad, hands full of popcorn and drinks, looking for me in the dark. He went all the way to the front of the theater and then turned around. I got up from my seat and moved away from the wheezing man into the aisle. I was relieved to see my father, but as he moved closer, I could tell he was pissed.

"Who were you sitting with," he asked way too loudly in the quiet theater. "Do you know that man?"

"No," I said, trying to keep my voice down. "He just sat next to me."

"What do you mean, he just sat next to you? Why did you *let* him?"

"I didn't. He just sat there."

I couldn't believe that my dad thought I would let some weird old guy sit next to me like that. But at the same time I wondered, why *did* the old guy sit next to me? What made him think he could?

Stirring up this kind of desire in creepy old men made me feel profoundly undesirable, as if I was as creepy as they were. It didn't help that like many young gay men, I suffered through junior high and high school—the pube-sprouting years—without ever having someone I was attracted to become attracted to me. Sure, it didn't help that at one point I'd put on the "faggot fifteen," that extra layer of pudge that many gay teens acquire in order to put the whole issue of sexuality on pause. But even when I lost the weight, on a diet of pizza and menthol cigarettes, I still couldn't catch the eyes of the straight jocks, nerd boys, and rock-climbing guys that I nursed crushes on. This made me feel, at my core, that no one I liked would ever like me. It was impossible, like an apple falling upward from a tree. And this feeling stayed with me even after I fell in love with Seth and he told me how attractive I was over and over again. On one level, I believed him, but on a deeper level, I kept expecting his feelings to pass. It was like he was under some kind of spell, and one day he would surely wake up.

I had so many mixed feelings about what it meant to be looked at, and I thought maybe stripping could help me sort some of it out. Maybe I could figure out what my desirability was worth tangibly. Maybe I could use it for my own benefit.

The other thing that attracted me to stripping was simply the opportunity to become the thing that fascinated me. Strippers had intrigued me since that first night at La Cage, and actually working as a stripper would let me understand how it actually felt to do it. It was like trying to get into the mind of someone you have a crush on, to understand them from the inside. This idea excited me.

But it also frightened me. Stripping wasn't illegal, but doing it could have undesirable consequences. How could I explain it to family, friends, and, most important, Seth, the guy I lived with and loved? He'd been cool about my fascination with strip clubs so far, but it would undoubtedly test his support to know that I was showing off my willy and letting customers play with it for a couple of bucks.

Then there was school to think about. Even though I taught two of my own classes, I wasn't really an employee. I was still a graduate student. I didn't know what rights I had or how I would find out about them. Somehow I didn't think it would work to go to the chair of my department and say, "I have this friend who, like, goes here and teaches, and he's thinking about becoming a stripper and wants to know if that would, like, get him in trouble."

Plus, I had to think about my classmates and students, many of whom were old enough to venture into the strip clubs if so inclined. It was so hard to sort out.

But on the flip side, I was also worried about *not* stripping. Was Nico right—did I think I was "too good"? Or not good enough? It didn't seem like the type of thing I would do, but at twenty-seven I didn't want to be penned in by preconceived notions of who I was. So I made up my mind to strip—partly for research, partly because of a bunch of personal baggage, but most important to see how life might change if I exercised my right to bare ass.

8

Two days after dancing at the Follies for the first time, I rushed across the green courtyard of the University of Maryland, racing past the columned brick buildings and the kids playing hacky sack in order to make my 11:00 AM class. It was late March and the campus was beginning to get pretty again. Maryland is one of those places where you experience four fully realized seasons—scorching in summer, leaf-filled in fall, snowy in winter, and sun-dappled in spring.

Luckily—and a bit uncharacteristically—I was on time getting to the classroom, a big blank space that looked like it had been made over by a minimalist schoolmarm, with its brick walls washed in thick coats of white paint and white blinds hanging from the ceiling-high windows. The students, about two dozen, sat in tiny wooden seats with built-in desks, and rows of fluorescent lights glared from above. One of my first thoughts upon setting my books down was how much more flattering the dim lights were at the Follies.

Standing there in front of the students, I was fully dressed in a polo shirt and some khakis. There were two layers of cotton between my dick and the rest of the world, yet I felt more exposed here. Not in a "Here's my ass" way, but in the sense of "Who the fuck am I to be instructing anybody about anything?"

It was my second semester teaching, but I still felt like I was playing teacher in a community theater production of college life. At any moment I expected a megaphone-wielding director to step in the class, shake his head, and yell, "No, no, no . . ."

It didn't help that my teaching had already come under attack. The course I'd been assigned to teach was called "Introduction to American Studies," but I was allowed to tailor it around my own research interests. I focused mine on gay and lesbian history. I wanted to show my students that there were gay people long before Ellen came out of the closet or Norman, Pedro, and Dan moved into their respective *Real World* houses. Yet this arguably noble goal bit me on the ass, and not in a hurts-so-good kind of way.

During the second week of my first semester teaching, an article ran in a national conservative newspaper condemning my class as an example of all that was wrong and too liberal about higher education. It turned out that one of the paper's reporters had been tipped off about the content of my course and snuck in the first class in order to snag a copy of my syllabus. The moment this hit the news, I received support from all fronts and my department backed me fully, but still it wasn't the way I wanted to kick off my teaching career. I was nervous enough simply standing in front of the class, and this incident increased my anxiety.

I began having panic attacks. During class I would be focused as much on what I was saying as I was on trying to control my face from twitching and my hands from shaking. I mostly did a good job at masking these reactions, but the one thing I couldn't stop was a profuse sweating condition I developed. It started the moment I put on clothes after getting out of the shower. By the time I got to school, my shirt would be completely drenched under each arm. I had to wear multiple layers—undershirts, sweaters, jackets—even when it was warm in order to hide what was going on. It was so fucked up. I had tried to teach a subject I was comfortable with and it had the effect of making me profoundly uncomfortable.

I'd wanted to connect my personal and intellectual lives, but they had never felt more separate. This became especially clear one day when one of my students, a star member of the wrestling team, visited me in my office to tell me how fascinating he found all the gay stuff. As he talked, he leaned farther and farther back in his chair, which was only a few inches away from mine. He spread his legs, bare in a pair of loose gym shorts, and I could see his blue-and-white boxers peek out from around his thigh. The longer we talked, the more he reclined, until his knee lightly pressed against mine. All we needed was some wacka-do, wacka-do music, and it would've been the perfect beginning to a really hot porn scene. But the funny thing about this was that I felt nothing, not the slightest bit of desire.

Here was a guy who perfectly fulfilled my jock fetish, an ideal young male specimen—one you'd want to clone, commission a sculpture of, or just fuck silly. Yet I felt none of the stirrings that I might feel if I saw him on the streets. Nor did I reflexively grab for dollar bills as I might have if I spotted him in a strip club.

Now don't get me wrong, all of this was exactly as it should've been. Boundaries are important in teaching, and I was glad I wasn't lusting after a student. But at the same time, I didn't know if I really wanted a job where I had to check my sexuality—such a major part of who I am—at the door. I was unsure how long I could sustain such a splintered life.

Stripping provided me a corrective to this. It gave me a platform to express my sexuality in a freeing, over-the-top way. But I didn't know if it would undo all that I had worked for in my career. I had to talk to my academic adviser about it, especially since I planned to write about my experiences in my dissertation.

"So what do you think?" I asked my adviser and strongest on-campus supporter, Dr. Parks. We were sitting in her office. A black baby doll smiled at me from a bookcase.

"You feel that you have to do it in order to get closer to your subjects?" she asked, leaning in close.

"Yeah," I answered. "How can I continue to gain their trust if I'm not willing to try it myself? That's like me saying that I'm 'too good' to do it or something."

"Well, it's a good idea in terms of the research. But it's also a risk. Academia can be a protective place, but it can also be very conservative."

"I know, but I feel like it's something I have to do. It's important, and I'm willing to accept the consequences. That's why I did it the first time without telling you. It's my decision and I'll take the responsibility."

"Well, make sure you're careful."

"Oh, I will be," I said, making a promise that would prove almost impossible to keep.

This conversation with my adviser was the second important talk that I'd had about stripping. The first had been with Seth before I said yes to working at the Follies.

"Just be clear on why you're doing it," he said as we changed the sheets on our bed one Sunday afternoon. We'd recently made a decision to be more diligent about housework since we were now living in our dream apartment—or at least the first we didn't share with creatures that crawled on multiple legs and kept low to the floor.

"What do you mean by *that*?" I asked, making sure I punctuated the last word with a sizable amount of attitude.

"You're doing it because you want to do it."

"I'm doing it because I need to do it for my research," I protested.

"Whatever. I don't want to fight about it," he said.

These conversations, with my adviser and with Seth, were the ones I had to have, but there were other talks I chose not to have—like with my parents. I never even considered telling them. I wasn't ashamed of what I was doing, and they both knew that I did research on strippers. But I felt there was no way to tell them and then expect them not to worry. It would put an undue burden on them and I didn't want to do that.

I needed a temporary reprieve from all of their best hopes and wishes. It wasn't that I didn't appreciate their concern—and of course, I had nothing but respect for the people who banged "privates" to make me. But I had to find out what my life meant for me. I wanted my epitaph to say more than "He Never Embarrassed His Parents."

Not telling "the folks" posed a number of problems, though. My father still lived in the area and we got together on weekends at least a couple of times a month, so it was hard to explain why I was less available.

My mom lived out of state, but we talked several times a day. How was I going to answer regular questions like "What's going on?" or "Have any plans for the weekend?" I didn't want to lie, but I had to be creative with the truth.

(Oddly enough, another person who I never told I was stripping was the very person who talked me into it: Nico. He disappeared from the scene shortly after our last conversation. At the time, I found it jarring the way people at the clubs would abruptly come and go. But I soon got used to it.)

After my first day at the Follies, I started working there about two Sundays a month. I liked the Follies because the dancers were treated about as professionally as you can be when your job description amounts to strip, play with yourself, let others play with you, repeat. We were even called "artists" in the contract we had to sign, as in "*Artist* will perform five shows per day. *Artist* is to be stripped of all clothing within four minutes of the beginning of the solo performance and for the entire finale," and "*Artist* will conduct himself in an orderly and professional manner at all times, including, but not limited to, proper hygiene during the course of this contract and proper dress when not performing."

I also liked the Follies because it offered some degree of privacy. Though the theater was a local landmark—it hosted gay civic awards ceremonies in the seventies—it was long past its prime in terms of popularity. The Follies customers weren't your average clubgoers. These were older guys who were there to watch porn, fondle strippers, and get laid in the back room. It wasn't likely that I'd see anybody I knew at the Follies, and if I did, their being there would say as much about them as my presence said about me.

I worked at the Follies for the entire spring 1996 semester, using my time between sets to prepare for classes or grade papers, red pen in hand. For the most part, things came off without a hitch and I was able to keep stripping separate from the other aspects of my life, except when my mother made a last-minute decision to come to D.C. on Mother's Day weekend, and I had already signed up to work that Sunday. I told her in advance that I'd only be able to hang out with her on Saturday because I had something important to do for school on Sunday. This wasn't really a lie. Nevertheless, things were weird from the moment she arrived.

We hooked up at my grandmother's house and decided to head out for coffee. I took her to the Starbucks in Dupont Circle, the queer mecca of D.C. We had just gotten out of the car and were walking to the coffeehouse when someone called out, "Hey, Craig." I immediately panicked. The voice was coming from a complete stranger in a hooded sweatshirt and baseball cap standing directly in front of us. I was sure it was someone who recognized me from the Follies. I had been stupid enough to use my real name when dancing, and now I was exposed. The stranger made eye contact with me, smiled flirtatiously, and kept walking.

"Do you know him?" my mom asked curiously.

My mind scrambled for ways to explain why this guy knew my name. He was too old to be a student, and my mother knew my boyfriend was Seth.

"No," I answered, trying to be casual. "I've never seen him in my life. I have no idea how he knows my name."

"It's on your jacket," my mother said, pointing to the large embroidered "Craig" on the auto mechanic's jacket I'd been wearing all spring.

"Oh," I said, not sure if this was the real reason he knew my name or not.

The next day—Mother's Day—I felt guilty that instead of spending time with my mother, I was getting paid to be felt up in a dark, smelly movie theater. I called her between every set, saying that I was taking a study break. But I felt like a liar. It was the first time since I started stripping that I wondered if I was doing the right thing.

9

Once I finished the spring semester, after final exams had been given and grades turned in, I decided to throw myself fully into stripping. The Follies featured dancers only on weekends—and they liked to rotate guys around—so I knew that if I wanted to work more I had to start dancing at one of the other clubs.

I chose Secrets, located two doors down from the Follies. This strip club, which showed off some of the best male bodies in town, was one half of a larger club that also featured drag shows. The drag side of the club was called Ziegfield's (pronounced *Zig-felds,* like the legendary Ziegfeld Follies). The part-stripper/part-drag vibe made the whole place like the physical manifestation of a vaudeville Mr. Lady act.

The drag show was overseen by a campy, glam wunderkind named Ella Fitzgerald. Born Donnell Robinson, he grew up in Warrenton, Virginia—a small farm town about an hour from D.C. His mother, who was a domestic, used to take in white folks' laundry on the side, and little Donnell would often sneak away blouses and shirts to play dress-up. He'd wait until everyone was asleep, then put on women's clothes and use a pair of stockings for hair. Sometimes he'd tie the stocking legs together in a braid; other times he'd pin them up in a nylon bouffant.

In 1975, Donnell left the farm with little more than a stack of Diana Ross 45's and a new polyester dress from Montgomery Ward. His destination: D.C. This is where he created his Ella persona. "In that era, in the seventies, anybody that did drag had to pick a celebrity's name," Ella once told me. "It was tradition. There was a Lucille Ball and a Marlo Thomas and an Elizabeth Montgomery, all the actresses."

Ella worked his way up through the ranks of the local drag scene, and on July 4, 1980, he got his big chance hosting a weekly drag show at a new club called Ziegfield's. Four years later, *Washingtonian* magazine named him best female impersonator.

By the time I started working at Secrets, Ella was a genuine local gay institution. Gone were the days when she used to stuff her bra with birdseed and dirty socks. She now used silicone implant bags that a nurse friend gave her. She also had an arsenal of great lady wigs and contacts in sea green and blue.

I wanted to work at Secrets because it had a laid-back vibe. I'd never seen dancers there yelled at by bartenders or management, and unlike at some of the other clubs, dancers didn't have to pick up empty glasses and beer bottles or take out the trash at the end of the night. I preferred my stripping less "blue collar," more "fire engine red Speedo."

Most important, though, I decided to work at Secrets because I didn't have to dance solely on top of a bar. Dancing on a bar terrified me. I lacked the grace of the boys who seemed to glide past a land mine of bottles, glasses, and threatening wet spots, and I knew I wouldn't be able to work the bar into my performance like this guy I once saw who stirred a drink with his cock. I just knew I'd end up either falling on my ass or getting someone's crotch wet, not because of my sensual moves but due to a foot-launched cocktail. Secrets offered a variety of different dancing areas in addition to the bar. There was a stage and about three sturdy raised platforms throughout the club. Dancers rotated among the various areas. I knew I'd have to log some bar time, but at least it would be limited.

The first weekend after school ended, I started at Secrets. I didn't even need to audition because a bunch of my Follies regulars put in a good word for me. I have no idea what the customers said; all I know is that the manager told me I could start anytime because I'd been "highly recommended."

I worked four nights a week, Thursday to Sunday: nine to two on Thursdays and Sundays, nine to three on Fridays and Saturdays. I danced in twenty-minute shifts and got paid $50 a night plus whatever I made in tips. If I walked out with at least $100 in my pocket, I was happy.

Working so regularly changed everything for me. The block, which could sometimes feel threatening with its pushy panhandlers and frequent car alarm squalls, now seemed homey. There was one older, needle-thin black man, Bobby, who would meet me at my car each time I arrived at work. I'd give him a couple of bucks to watch my car and I never had a problem.

One night I was running late and there was almost no place to park, so I had to pull my car into the middle of a deep mud puddle. In order to get to dry pavement, I squeezed out of the passenger door and climbed over the car. I was crawling on top of my hood when someone jumped out of the shadows and rushed toward me. I quickly slid down the back of my car and got to my feet ready for a fight. But then I saw it was Bobby.

"Oh, hey," I said. "You scared the shit out of me."

"My fault," he said. "I thought someone was fuckin' with my man's car."

"No problem," I said, handing him some bills. I was stunned that he took his role as a car protector so seriously. I always figured he just took my bucks and ran.

"Stay safe tonight," I told him.

"You, too, my brother," he said, walking back beyond the streetlights. "You, too."

This exchange with Bobby was an example of how I was seeing many things about stripping and the whole scene in a new way.

I spent much of those first few weeks at Secrets trying to find my comfort zone. It was about figuring out what kind of stripper I was going to be. Would I be one of those flash-dancing pole spinners, or would I follow in the paths of those showboys who had a trademark shtick, picking up a dollar with their ass cheeks or placing a quarter on their hard dick and then flicking it out into the crowd? Each of these options held its appeal, but then again, I knew they would never work for me. Spinning around the pole seemed too much like a sport, and since I was always the kid who couldn't pull off even the most elementary magic trick in grade school, I figured any type of razzle-dazzle stunts were out of the question. Basically, I opted to be the guy who comes onstage, quickly takes off all his clothes as if taking part in some emergency preparedness drill, gets a hard-on, and then wanders around absently playing with his dick until someone walks up with a tip. I did so little dancing or any other type of movement that a lot of customers thought I was straight—which was not necessarily a bad thing when it came to tips. Most gay guys have nursed a straight-boy fantasy at some point in their lives.

Although I was a little nervous about my performance at first, I also learned that there was almost no way to make a mistake as long as I adhered to the general guidelines of the club, which at the time were limited to "Don't yawn onstage" and "Don't let them stick your dick in their mouths."

On one of my first nights, I was dancing onstage when a short, bald guy walked over to me. I moved closer to him and, misjudging our relative distance, poked him in the center of his forehead with my hard dick. Everybody around us started laughing. I kneeled down. "I'm really sorry," I said, embarrassed. But then I saw that the bald man was laughing, too. He spent the rest of the night trying to "accidentally" get me to knock him in the head again.

Finally, I said to him, "Isn't this getting a little old?"

"Never," he asked, laughing and stuffing a wad of dollars in my sock. "So, what's your name?"

"Craig," I said, kneeling down. "What's yours?"

"Michael," he said, with one hand on my cock. "Are you new here?"

"I just started working here, but I've been working at the Follies for a couple of months."

"Well, you're quite good at what you do."

"Thanks."

"Hey," he said. "Do you mind if I rub your ass? You have a beautiful butt."

"OK, but no fingers."

"Promise," he said, crossing his fingers.

Then I turned around and bent over on my knees as he rubbed my ass cheeks. I let him do this for about a minute, then I turned back around.

"Wow, that was amazing," he said. "You're a beautiful guy."

"Glad to be of service," I said with a smile.

"Now, one last thing," he added, tipping me another few bucks. "Will you hit me on the head with your cock again?"

"I guess," I said, before tapping him on his bald dome again. All his friends started clapping.

"Thanks," he said. "No bullshit. You've made my whole night, my week even."

"No problem," I said, giving him a hug.

The idea that I could make some guy so happy by simply hitting him over the head with my dick and letting him rub my butt gave me a rush. There was something appealing about the whole experience of letting a stranger feel my body. It was all about sensation, skin on skin. And the surprising thing is that for the most part, it didn't feel gross or sleazy. In fact, the whole thing made me feel strangely powerful, like I'd been given a new way to communicate.

That night, when I arrived home, Seth was already asleep. But as I climbed into bed, after taking a shower, he turned over in his sleep and put his arms around me. I lay there and thought about the lyrics to one of my favorite songs by the seventies soul sister act the Emotions: "Blessed that be the ties that bind." I knew that what Seth and I had was real, grounded, tight, binding.

But I also knew that there was something equally real going on with me and some of my customers, like Michael. I felt the pleasure I gave to them. There was even something pure and innocent about the way they so nakedly exposed their desires, the way they so openly derived pleasure from someone they thought was beautiful. Sure, the whole thing was based around the exchange of cash, but that didn't solely define what went on or how the customers felt about it. Money was simply how each story began.

Everything at the club was far more complex than I even imagined before I started dancing myself. This became especially clear as I had the chance to get close to some of my fellow dancers, my comrades in this brotherhood of boys gone wild. Between sets, we'd shoot the shit in the Secrets dressing room, which was really a large, restaurant-quality kitchen due to that goofy D.C. law requiring all bars to be fully equipped to serve food. The talk often ran to occupational hazards like how to keep your dick from chafing after being rubbed all night (most guys used Elbow Grease, but there was a small but vocal cocoa butter contingent) and how to stop those customers who try to stick their fingers up your ass (when you kneel down, sit on the heel of your foot). These discussions bonded us despite our differences. Some of us were gay; some were straight; others figured it out day by day, dollar by dollar. But we all had to grapple with what it meant to let other guys pay to ogle us and feel our business.

We were also aware that we were doing a job that many people thought was disgusting and degrading. But for most of us, it was a job choice like any other, amounting to a compromised negotiation among ideals, capabilities, and opportunities. The only difference was that stripping made you shockingly aware of the chasm that can exist between who you think you are and what you're willing to do for money.

The dressing room was filled with a constantly changing cast of characters, as guys started stripping, quit, disappeared, and then, more often than not, reappeared. ("I guess rent's due," I once overheard a customer remark upon a dancer's return to the scene.) There was Patrick, a sturdy All-American type who stripped on nights when he wasn't playing the lead in a local production of *Joseph and the Amazing Technicolor Dreamcoat,* and Puppyboy, a short, skinny guy who crawled along the bar on all fours, occasionally lifting his leg like he was taking a whiz. (This was all cute until one night he stuck his rump in a customer's face and accidentally let out a short, sputtering fart. At that moment, he quickly lost the four-legged shtick, hopped to his feet, and dashed back to the dressing room, red-faced.)

Then there was Sid, a straight bleached-blond punk and unapologetic hustler known for offering tips on topics like giving a professional blow job. ("Get the money in advance, then try to get the guy to wear a condom; if he insists that you suck him without a condom, tell him you have cold sores.") And Danny, a sort of gyrating cautionary tale, who was returning to dancing after a breakup with a longtime boyfriend. Fifteen years earlier, a boyish Danny was the hottest guy on the block, and he had a reputation for over-the-top temper tantrums. One time he hurled a shot glass across a club and shattered a full-length mirror. "I'm too old to pull that shit now," he told me one night, while stepping into a jock strap. "Still have my twenty-seven-inch waist, though."

The key to getting along at the club was learning to live with other people's contradictions. It didn't take long to realize that a person's stated sexual orientation had nothing to do with how he might act at the club or the sex he might have for money. "Straight" and "gay" lost meaning for me. I soon barely noticed when, say, Steve—a married, blond, surfer-looking dude who liked to show off pictures of his towheaded daughters dressed for church—got into a customer's car and soon had his head bobbing up and down on the driver's lap.

Money was the all-purpose justifier for almost any type of behavior. It helped many straight guys explore homo aspects of their sexuality without having to own up to boy-on-boy stirrings. Just as frisky, sexually ambivalent frat boys use the excuse "I was so drunk last night," straight dancers could do almost anything with another guy as long as bills were exchanged.

The money also helped assuage outraged girlfriends, wives, and other family members. A straight dancer once told me about the time his mother caught him putting together a construction worker costume—tool belt, hat, G-string—for a stripper-of-the-month contest. She was shocked to find out that her son was entering a nude dancing contest at a gay bar.

"But Ma," he said, "first prize is five hundred dollars."

"Five hundred dollars," his mother said. "You should've told me. I would've *made* you a costume."

The other thing we talked about in the dressing room was the customers. Because we were in D.C., there was a lot of speculation—often false, sometimes true—about who our customers were: this one's a congressman; that one's a White House aide; the fat guy over there is a prominent *Washington Post* critic.

We placed the other customers in categories: The good kinds of customers were the "regulars," who could always be counted on; "sugar daddies," who tipped big and bought us gifts; and "moms," who did things like bake us brownies and cookies and give us birthday and other holiday cards. The bad kinds of customers included "the watchers," who just stood along the back wall staring but never tipping, and the jerks who assumed they knew something about our lives just because we were strippers.

One night a short guy with a pencil-thin mustache came up to me at the stage, tipped me, and said, "I want to eat your ass and then fuck you all day long."

"Thanks," I answered, "but I have a boyfriend."

"That's too bad. I could do a lot for you."

"Oh, really?"

"Yeah," he said, before explaining how he was a supervisor in one of the local school districts.

I felt like saying, "That's OK, I'm actually a Ph.D. student at one of the most prestigious state research institutions on the East Coast, thanks." But I didn't. I quickly learned that telling a customer—almost any customer—that I was in grad school was a sure way to not get tipped, so I usually just kept it general and said I was a "student."

"By the way, what name are you using here," the pencil-mustache man asked.

"Craig," I said. "Always Craig—that's my real name."

"Oh, I believe you," he said with a dramatic eye roll, "truly I do."

As he walked away, I could distinctly see his lips mouth the words "full of shit."

But as annoying as these patronizing customers could be, the most off-putting customers were the "fetish guys," simply because they gave us the creeps. One guy liked to rub us with a pair of worn acid-washed jeans that he brought with him and carried in his hands. Another always tried to wiggle his fingers under our arms and along our sides. We dubbed him "Mr. Tickles."

Not all of the customers were cringe-worthy, though. There were some who I even looked forward to seeing. On one of my first weekends working at Secrets, I stepped out on the stage and saw Dave among the customers. I hadn't told him I was dancing and when he spotted me, he did an eye-popping double take worthy of a Daffy Duck cartoon.

"So when did this happen?" he asked when he walked over to me. He put a couple of ones in my sock and I knelt down.

"A couple of weeks now."

"Well, *how* did it happen?"

"You know, I'd always been curious and I finally just thought I'd give it a try. Besides, Nico dared me, so I couldn't not do it then."

"Do the people at your school know?"

"Not really. My adviser knows, but nobody else. And certainly not my students."

"Yeah, I could imagine that would be pretty awkward."

"You could say that."

He looked at my cock, which was beginning to get hard.

"Do you mind?" he asked, looking down at it.

"It's what I'm here for," I answered.

He worked on me a little while, and as I grew in his hands, he looked up and laughed nervously.

"Now see, this is something that I could never do," he said.

"Really?"

"Yeah, I mean even when I was younger I couldn't deal with people touching me unless I wanted them to."

"It's not that hard," I said and then realized my word choice didn't quite match my erectile state. "I mean, it's not that difficult."

"It certainly seems like you've taken to it."

"Well, I've spent enough time watching. And besides, how difficult is it to get a hard-on and stand around?"

"True," he said. "Hey, have you seen Peter around?"

"He's on the next set," I told him. He tipped me again and I moved on to another customer.

Since I started dancing, Peter and I had been spending a lot of time together, talking before and after work and between sets. He was by far one of the quirkiest guys that I ever worked with. Some of the other dancers didn't like him because he took a hall monitor approach to stripping. He turned off dressing room lights when no one was in there and cleaned up after other dancers. One time at the Follies, Peter and I were working with this chain-smoking

French Canadian guy, Marcel, who left cigarette butts all over the dressing room floor. At the end of the night, Peter swept up every one.

"My mom and dad used to own a corner store," Peter explained, "and so every place I work, I respect it like it was my own."

He even used this corner store approach when dealing with customers. "My parents taught me to treat every customer with respect and try to please everybody," he said. "You can't always do that, but you can try. I know they didn't have stripping in mind, but just in general."

A self-described "scruffy farm boy," Peter grew up near Rehoboth Beach in Delaware. One summer day, Peter, who was just out of high school, was working at an umbrella rental stand on the beach when the owner of a local gay club offered him $100 to dance at the club that night. Peter was intrigued. "I was always interested in modeling and I looked at this like live modeling," he said.

That night, Peter showed up at the club in one of his high school swim team Speedos.

"You don't have a G-string?" the club owner asked.

"No," Peter said.

"Oh, what the hell. Just wedgie up the back and make it look like a thong."

When Peter told me this story, as we sat on the dressing room's facing steel countertops, I asked him how he felt dancing for the first time. "Well, it was weird. Not so much the dancing. But I had never been to a gay bar before and I didn't know about things like drag queens and leather and handcuffs and all that stuff. It was all new to me, but I was trying to be nice about it."

"So I guess you're not gay?"

"I was classifying myself as asexual at the time."

"You've never been attracted to guys?"

"It was always off and on. I'd think about it. Sometimes I'd go to this water park and walk in front of guys, even if they seemed totally straight, just to see if they'd check me out. It's like being on the verge of something but then when it is about to happen, maybe you don't want it after all. Something like that."

Peter was such a hit with customers at the Rehoboth club that the owner kept inviting him back. One evening, some vacationers told Peter that he should check out the D.C. clubs. Peter thought it was a good idea because he didn't have any job prospects come fall and he knew he could crash with some family members who lived outside the city.

"Does your family know you strip?" I asked.

"No, and they're never going to know. I don't think they would understand. A few years ago, I wouldn't have been able to understand it myself. But I figure that what I'm doing is not costing people their lives. It's not drugs. It's just a different kind of entertainment."

10

As the summer weeks passed, I became more serious about my job as a boy, if not for sale, then at least for controlled-access rental. I bought new outfits and paraphernalia: jock straps, Speedos, G-strings, and a cool double-loop cock ring that separated my dick from my balls, making it stick out like a pistol when hard. I carried all this stuff with me in my Nike duffel bag, which also included lotion, breath mints (not gum, which was frowned upon), lemon-scented Wet Ones for quick freshening-ups, and Elbow Grease.

I developed a ritual for getting ready for work. I tried to be home from wherever I was during the day by 6 PM. This allowed me to eat, shower, and shave before leaving for work around 8 PM. Shaving, of course, entailed more than just running a razor over my face. I kept my chest bare, and I'd shave the shaft of my dick to make it look bigger and all around my balls so that they wouldn't get sweaty and stink.

Before leaving for the club, I'd check out my shaving job in a full-length mirror that I kept in the closet. The mirror was in the closet instead of hanging on the wall because the mirror was mine and Seth was the official hanger-of-things in the relationship. He kept promising to put it up for me, but never got around to it. In a way, this slab of reflective glass summed up the main difference between Seth and me. He'd never owned a full-length mirror; I couldn't live without one.

All of my preparation before work was in the service of trying to make myself come off as desirable as possible. Most people have similar grooming rituals when getting ready for a date on a Saturday night. The difference is a stripper has to be alluring and attractive day after day for several hours at a time, a feat that takes considerable effort to maintain and is sometimes tricky to pull off.

Even taking a dump at work—a thought that terrifies many cubicle dwellers—was particularly problematic for those of us who spent a large chunk of the workday spreading our ass cheeks in a customer's face. The extent of this dilemma became clear to me one night at Secrets when Donnie, a fellow dancer who I'd become friendly with, came into the dressing room looking distressed. "Craig, I have to sh-iii-t," he said, bouncing up and down and holding his stomach. It was a strange image. Donnie was a muscular black man with a pumped-up chest, mountainous biceps, and a thick, round booty, but at this moment, he was acting like a little kid.

"Go ahead then," I said, not quite realizing why this obvious solution wasn't apparent to him.

"I c-aaa-n't," he said, stretching his vowels like they were a lifeline, the only thing keeping him from dropping a turd that very instant.

"Why not?"

"I can't shit in the bathrooms here. All the customers are in there. It'd be embarrassing."

He had a point. It certainly didn't add to a dancer's allure to be seen coming out of a funky stall. Besides, there was always so much commotion in the Secrets bathrooms: customers walking in and out; stall doors swinging open and slamming shut; guys flirting at the urinals while staring at one another's pissing cocks. It was not the kind of place where you could comfortably come in with a cup of joe and a folded copy of the *Washington Post*, sit down, and get your bowels a-movin'.

Donnie lived too far away, so there was no time for him to get home and back in the fifteen minutes before our next set. But there was enough time to go to a large, gay dance club nearby. This offered more anonymity. Donnie didn't have a car, so he asked me to be the wheels man. In order to preserve the intestinal dignity of my fellow dancer, I became an accomplice in "Operation Shit."

Once agreeing on the plan, we quickly changed out of our stripper gear and started making our exit. As we headed out of Secrets, the doorman stopped us.

"Where are you two going?" he said, eyeing us suspiciously. "Your sets are coming up."

"To get food," I answered at the same time Donnie said, "We need cigarettes." It was like a cheesy sitcom farce. I thought the doorman was going to ask more questions, but he was soon back to looking at his crossword puzzle. No one expected strippers to make sense.

We reached the car. Donnie jumped in the passenger seat and we were off. One block passed, then two. We crossed a bustling intersection, turned a corner, and pulled into the circular driveway of Tracks, the city's busiest gay dance club, which was also the place where Seth and I really connected for the first time.

Donnie jumped out and exchanged some words with the club's bouncer, who I assumed was a friend. He disappeared into the club. I watched the trendy young gay boys gathered out front, smiling, talking to friends, their hair shining under the streetlights. Is that what I looked like that night I came here with Seth, so fresh and full of anticipation?

These guys weren't spending their night standing on platforms, swapping stories with their straight-boy coworkers, and hustling older guys out of cash. Their worst worry of the night would be farting with a lover in bed later, not shitting onstage. Yet somehow I was glad that I was where I was instead of where they were. I didn't know why, but I wouldn't have wanted it any other way.

A few minutes passed. I looked at the clock, and got nervous because we had to be back in four minutes. Nevertheless, I realized that proper hygiene, however time-consuming, was important at a time like this.

I looked back at the door and Donnie came rushing out with a notably lighter step. "Let's go," he said, jumping in the car. We made it back to the club. The doorman looked up. We had no food or cigarettes with us, but all he said was, "You're cutting it close tonight." I figured he thought we had just done a duo show and serviced a trick at the porn theater next door, something that was not an uncommon occurrence.

Donnie and I got back to the kitchen for a quick change. Already the dancers from the previous set were making their way off the bar, stage, and boxes. I got my pants off, grabbed my cock ring, and accidentally pinched a wad of ball skin in the snap while trying to put it on. "Fuck," I yelled, taking off the cock ring and throwing it back in my gym bag.

I rushed out of the kitchen, two minutes late for my set. The dancer who I was replacing onstage rolled his eyes at me. At Secrets, you weren't allowed to leave your position until another dancer replaced you. I looked around and fortunately didn't see the manager, who had been giving people shit about being late. Within minutes, things got really busy and I had a line of guys waiting to stroke my cock. Thankfully, I was able to get a hard-on even without the cock ring. Tips were coming in fast. It was gonna be a good night.

As I dropped to my knees and let another guy tug my dick back and forth, I glanced over to see Donnie kneeling on the bar in front of one of his regulars. He was politely nodding at whatever the customer was saying when he spotted me looking over at him. He lifted his hand and wiped his brow, the universal sign of relief.

11

One of the more surprising things about my time at Secrets was that I soon became one of the most popular dancers, consistently making more than $100 a night and pulling in my own flock of regulars. I cornered the market for racially ambiguous boys-next-door. The funny thing is that both of my parents are black—and you have to go *Roots*-in' back to my great-grandmother on my father's side to find a white person—but my toffee-colored skin makes my race hard for people to place. (When it later came to scheduling at one of the other clubs, I was the tragic mulatto of dick dancers—too brown for "Vanilla Shake Mondays," not brown enough for "Hot Chocolate Wednesdays.")

This ambiguity mostly worked to my advantage. Depending on the customer's taste, I could be a swarthy white ethnic, a charming mocha latte poster child for race mixing, a tan Filipino, or almost any variation of Latino.

The only problems generally arose when I told customers I was black. As one white guy once said to me before moving on to another dancer, "I liked you better when I thought you were Latino."

The racial dynamics of the clubs gave me mixed feelings. Sometimes I'd think, "What is a nice middle-class black boy like me doing showing off his dick for old white men? Is the Secrets stage just an updated auction block? Did Martin march in the streets and get shot down for this? Did Sister Rosa stay at the front of the bus so I could shake my ass in the back of the club?" It was a conundrum.

But despite these reservations, I knew I couldn't stop dancing. I didn't want to stop, and I figured that at heart, freedom was about having the choice to do whatever you wanted to do. I was convinced that there were still things I needed to learn about myself by stripping, and I was committed to seeing where this adventure would lead me.

Standing naked onstage at Secrets, I was within a dozen miles of all the landmarks of my life—the hospital where I was born, the concrete government block where my father worked, the campus where I taught and went to school, and the houses that both sets of grandparents bought back in the sixties, their own hard-won pieces of one of the most powerful cities in the world. Yet despite this physical proximity, it seemed like I was worlds away from how I started life, trying to desperately embody the phrase "young, gifted, and black" and come off smart and "articulate," as white folks would sometimes remark.

My Afro stood upright and rounded on my head, which I

held up high as I sat in integrated elementary school classrooms representing the race. I knew all my black history facts, learned dutifully from constant practice with flash cards; gave school reports on George Washington Carver and Dr. Charles Drew; and could recite passages from Dr. Martin Luther King Jr.'s "I Have a Dream" speech when called upon at family functions to impress sididdy relatives. When people likened me to Michael Evans of *Good Times,* I would pump my fist in the air and say, "Right on!"

Perhaps because of these comparisons, I pursued acting, joining Howard University's Children's Theatre. I even won the lead role in *Rumple,* a black retelling of "Rumpelstiltskin." It was supposed to blow up like *The Wiz.* But *Rumple* failed to catch on and the world never got to hear me sing-rap about spinning straw into gold.

When I was in junior high, I became a regular on *The Sunshine Store,* a children's TV show on the local NBC affiliate. I played the friendly neighborhood black kid who came in the store and learned life lessons from the middle-aged white store owner. In that way, the premise was similar to *Diff'rent Strokes* or *Webster* except I didn't get adopted.

About a year after that, I became an anchor on a kids' TV magazine, *Newsbag.* The gig was mostly uneventful save for the time when an appearance by Brooke Shields, in town promoting some children's charity, coincided with me getting my first zit. It was a bright red number that wedged itself in the crevice around my right nostril, and it made me so self-conscious that I couldn't get up the nerve to ask Brooke what her *Blue Lagoon* costar Christopher Atkins was *really* like.

These kinds of thoughts made it increasingly hard for me to deny to myself that I was gay. There was no way around it—that poster of shirtless Soloflex model Scott Madsen was not on my wall to encourage me to exercise. But this truth made me angry. I couldn't risk letting my friends and family find out about me. I felt like I was walking around with a live grenade. If I accidentally dropped it, my whole world could explode.

This anger made me act out in all sorts of ways. By the time I was around fifteen, I had shed any pretense of being a model middle-class black kid. It was the *Cosby Show* era, and instead of trying to ape Theo Huxtable, with his corny high-top-fade–wearing self, I was shooting for Lisa Bonet, nude on the cover of *Rolling Stone* and fucking in chicken blood in *Angel Heart*. I bleached my hair, developed a two-pack-a-day Yves Saint Laurent menthol cigarette habit, and skipped almost as many classes as I attended. In high school, I might've been voted "Least Likely to Amount to Much of Anything"—that is, if I'd actually finished high school. I dropped out and worked full time as a telemarketer for Time-Life Books.

When I wasn't on the phone hawking the Old West series to retirees and shut-ins, I was hanging out with my friend Matthew, a cool-ass white boy who loved Afrika Bambaataa and Chaka Khan and had hip-hop lyrics written on his white Converse high-tops. Matthew and I were primarily obsessed with two things: music and *The Young and the Restless.* That's all we talked about as we walked around D.C. late at night or drove out to the Maryland suburbs where his mother worked behind the counter at 7-Eleven. Once, when Matthew went to L.A., he brought me back an ornament stolen from the *Young and the Restless* set.

For the most part, we didn't discuss a lot of personal stuff, but one time when we were talking about gay people, I told Matthew that I couldn't imagine kissing another guy. He looked me in the eyes and said, "Of course you can," recognizing something in me that I wasn't ready to acknowledge.

Not long afterward, I moved to New York City with Matthew and some friends and became a featured dancer on *Club MTV*, hosted by Downtown Julie Brown. It wasn't so much that I was a good dancer as that the casting people liked my look—hair dyed blond, black leather jacket, Doc Martens, and jeans. (Later I switched to a style that mostly consisted of Calvin Klein boxers worn over long johns, and one of the producers pulled me aside and asked if I wouldn't mind returning to my original style.) I liked being on the show because I thought it would launch me into the limelight. Fame would solve all my problems, because when you were famous you could do anything—dance in your underwear like Madonna, show your ass crack on an album sleeve like Prince, or most important, be gay like Boy George or the dude with the high-pitched voice from Bronski Beat.

At downtimes during taping, I imagined myself teaming with two other dancers and becoming the *Club MTV* version of Shalamar, the disco/R&B trio that sprang from the ranks of the *Soul Train* dancers. But the closest I got to that dream was staring up the back of ex–Shalamar member Jody Watley's hoop skirt as I danced behind her while she performed her hit "Looking for a New Love" on the show.

When I wasn't taping *Club MTV,* I was hanging out as a part of the touring entourage of an Italian club diva named Nocera, who had a smash with an airy freestyle number called "Summertime, Summertime." We'd make our way through clubs all over New York, Jersey, and Philly. Nocera and her dancers would perform, my friend would collect the cash payments from the club owners, and I would sit backstage and use spit to wipe the scuffs off my Doc Martens. After a few months of this, I got bored and restless. My life didn't seem to be going anywhere and I was pissed off about it.

I got in a fight with some of my roommates, threatened one of them with a steak knife (in a move that was *way* more drama queen than sadistic slasher, but still . . .), and was promptly and justifiably thrown out on my ass. With nowhere else to go, I returned home to my parents, who insisted that I take the G.E.D. and try to find a way to go to college. As I agreed to the arrangement, I started to visualize my dreams of having an exciting life swirling in the basin of a sink and then washing down the drain.

Matthew and I didn't talk much after that. He'd had his own falling-out with some of the roommates long before the knife incident, which caused him to flee the apartment and not tell anyone where he was going.

But about six months after I moved home, I unexpectedly received a handwritten note from Matthew in the mail. "If this letter gets to you somewhere in this burning world," he opened, "I have a feeling you can still relate." For five densely marked pages, Matthew revisited all of our favorite topics of conversation, telling me how he was awaiting a new Frankie Knuckles remix of Chaka Khan's "Ain't Nobody," going through a love/hate relationship with Whitney Houston's "One Moment in Time," and incensed over the direction of *The Young and the Restless.* ("That show suffered so much during the writers' strike— will it ever rebound?") Later, he stated: "Writing this letter to you makes me happy. Whatever happened to us? I miss talking to you, but somehow I know what you're thinking or want to convince myself that I know."

At the end of the letter, he wrote: "213 area code soon. Call me." But I never did. Once I started on the long path of going to school, being a good boy, and doing what my parents wanted me to, I couldn't look back and reconnect with someone who I'd shared so many crazy obsessions and dreams with. Still, every time I entered a new situation, I always remembered something he'd told me: "Craig, people will like you wherever you go."

The next time I heard anything about Matthew was years later while flipping through *Vanity Fair.* According to an article in the magazine, he had indeed moved to L.A. and transformed himself into conservative internet pundit Matt Drudge.

12

As I continued dancing at Secrets, I generally was able to keep my stripping life separate from my personal life and my school life. Seth came in once to see me work, but he didn't stay long. He said it made him uncomfortable, but we didn't discuss it much more than that. Another time, one of my college friends, who had since moved out of town, came into the bar. He knew I'd written about strippers for my master's thesis, but he had no idea that I'd started dancing.

When I saw him, I was kneeling on one of the platforms, my dick still hard from my last customer. He walked up to me, and for a moment I wondered if he was going to touch my dick, which—in the logic of the clubs—would've been weird because he was a friend, not a stranger. But instead he said, "Boy, you really know how to throw yourself into your research," and we both laughed.

By far the weirdest encounter I had with someone I knew, though, happened one Saturday night when I was onstage dancing—or to be more accurate, rapidly swaying—to one of my favorite songs, the club remix of Mariah Carey's "Fantasy."

I was really into it, getting lost in the lyrics ("seems so real but it's a fantasy . . . it's such a sweet fantasy") and wagging my cock from side to side to the beat, when I looked toward the door and spotted this guy, Doug, who was once in a graduate African-American history seminar with me. We made eye contact and he nervously looked away and raced to the drag side of the club.

"Oh, shit," I thought. I didn't even know this guy was gay and I wondered if he was going to spread what I did around school. My adviser was still the only person at the university who knew I danced, and while I didn't live in constant fear of exposure, as it might be portrayed in the Lifetime made-for-TV movie version of my life, I was anxious about what would happen if word really got out. I knew my adviser could protect me only so much. Even though stripping was legal, I knew that wouldn't count for much if I was up against conservative media pundits, overreacting parents, and nervous university officials. And because stripping and other forms of sex work are so controversial, I doubted that any gay or African-American organization would come to my aid if I got in hot water.

After my set finished, I got dressed and went to look for Doug in the audience for the drag show, but I couldn't find him. I wanted to gauge his reaction. I looked for him the whole night but never saw him.

When I got home, I emailed him: "Hey—were you at Secrets tonight by any chance?" I thought a coy approach was best.

The next morning, he answered: "Yeah, I thought that was you."

"Yep," I responded. "I've been working there this summer, doing ethnographic research for my dissertation. You should've said hi."

"Yeah, well, I wasn't sure it was you."

I figured he was lying about this. After all, I had seen the shock and recognition on his face, but I let it go. It didn't sound like he planned on outing me.

"No prob," I typed.

Aside from these encounters, I never saw anyone else I knew from school at Secrets. That was another reason why I liked working there. I didn't even consider dancing anywhere else until one day Danny came back into the kitchen/dressing room and said he needed to talk to me and another of the club's most popular dancers, Mikey, a twenty-one-year-old white bodybuilder who started stripping after he dropped out of college. "It just wasn't for me," Mikey explained.

Like many of the other boys who paraded their dangling and stiffened wares around the club, Mikey maintained he was straight, but he was unrestrained about his love for the job. He dug the schedule and he especially loved the money. "When I started, I was four thousand dollars in debt," he once told me. "Within three months, I had no debt, beaucoup new clothes and new jewelry, and I was on my way to putting a down payment on a new car."

Mikey didn't even mind getting felt on by a bunch of gay guys. "This is a muscle," he explained to me one night, flexing his baseball-sized biceps, "and this is a muscle," he continued, pointing toward his cock. "If a guy touches me here [his arm], they can touch me there [his cock]."

"What do you say if a customer asks if you're gay?" I asked him one night as we sat in the dressing room.

"Usually," he said, looking up from counting a stack of bills, "I'll tell them that I'm straight, but that I messed around with a few guys when I was in high school. That generally keeps them going."

Danny wanted to talk to us because the manager of Mr. P's, a gay dive in Dupont Circle, was looking for some guys to dance on Wednesdays, one of the nights when Secrets was closed. I felt a little uneasy about doing it because Mr. P's was located in the official gayborhood, so there was more of a chance to be seen by someone I knew. Mr. P's also had the reputation for a relatively rough clientele. There was no cover, so anyone could walk in off the street.

I was on the verge of saying no when Danny told me that they were paying $50 for two hours' work plus tips. I was taking Seth to see *Rent* on Broadway for his birthday, and this extra money would come in handy. Besides, Mikey readily accepted the offer, and I seldom passed on any opportunity to work with him. We were buddies of sorts. He told me about his girl problems; I quietly lusted after him.

The first night at Mr. P's started strangely. The club wasn't licensed for nudity so we had to keep our G-strings on and we couldn't play with ourselves. This left me feeling self-conscious because I had nothing to do with my hands.

Adding to my anxiety, they made us dance on a tiny bar located in a dark upstairs room. TINY. BAR. DARKNESS. The words triggered my near-constant fear of ASS ON FLOOR. But I thought I could stomach it for a couple of hours.

And I was looking forward to working with Mikey. A lot of dancers thought he was a prick, but he was always nice to me. As we stood naked in the upstairs employee bathroom that they made us use as a dressing room, I noticed him staring at me in the mirror. He stood there big, muscular, manly, and tan, while I looked short, fleshy, boyish, and pale.

"What the fuck are you looking at?" I said, jokingly.

"Oh nothing, just comparing," he said with a laugh.

"Fuck you," I said, shoving him playfully. "Get away from me."

"Don't worry, I may beat you in some ways, but definitely not if we're comparing cocks. You have me beat by a mile, or at least a couple of inches."

"Yeah, yeah," I said.

"No, seriously. We should give you a nickname or something, like 'The Little Boy with the Big Toy.' Or, I know, what about 'Li'l Big Chief'?"

"No thanks," I replied, secretly thrilled that he even

noticed my cock, much less wanted to give it a nickname.
I imagined this is what it was like to be on a football or bas-
ketball team and share a sort of casual, ass-baring, locker
room intimacy with other guys.

"Man Saber," Mikey offered.

"Nope."

He paused for a moment. "OK, I've got it," he said. "The
Weapon."

"That's better," I said, just as Danny came racing in the
room.

"Craig, you're on now. Mikey, you take the next set."

"OK," I said, pulling up my red G-string and following
him out the door and down the steps to the club.

"Mikey's so hot," I said to Danny as we walked down the
stairs.

"Yeah, I'd probably date his father," responded Danny,
who had a thing for older married men.

There were only a few customers at the bar, and the one
paying the most attention to me was an older guy with a
handlebar mustache. He especially liked it when I stood
over him and slowly bent down until my dick, bundled in
the pouch of a red G-string, nearly rested on the tip of his
nose.

I didn't recognize any of the customers from Secrets or
the Follies until I saw the infamous Mr. Tickles. He wore
his trademark trench coat and his face was flushed red as
always. In the past, Mr. Tickles had never tipped me and by
now I'd learned not to take this personally. I knew I wasn't
going to be every guy's type. But that night, Mr. Tickles

walked right up to where I was on the bar. I kneeled down in front of him. He put a couple of ones in my sock and proceeded to tickle me under each armpit. It felt weird and a little dry and scratchy. (You'd think a guy with a tickling fetish would keep his nails filed and invest in a good hand cream.) But I tried to muster a smile.

"Do you like to be tickled?" he asked in a squeaky, pinched voice.

"Oh yeah," I said, trying to inject my voice with pornlike conviction.

He kept tickling me for about thirty more seconds, and then he patted me on my calf and moved away without saying a word. I couldn't tell if he was a satisfied customer or a disappointed one.

When I told Danny about this, he said my failure to come off like a tickling enthusiast was a big financial mistake. "Honey, Mr. Tickles is one of the best tippers there is," he said, lacing up his black boots.

Danny claimed that he once went to Mr. Tickles's house to be tickle-tortured for an hour. His compensation: a round-trip plane ticket to the vacation destination of his choice. I never knew if I fully believed all of Danny's stories, but I figured that since he'd been doing this for longer than anyone else I knew, he'd earned the right to a few exaggerations.

After talking with Danny, I went back out for another set. I hadn't made as much money as I wanted to, so I was pleased to see Handlebar Mustache Man still at the bar. I'd given myself a nice fluffing in the bathroom, making my cock hard underneath the G-string. Feeling quite proud of my overstuffed red crotch pouch, I walked over to him, waited while he slipped some money in my sock, then slowly moved my package toward his face. He leaned his head back and opened his mouth. I flirtatiously moved closer. I figured that maybe he was like my Secrets regular Michael and wanted to get bopped in the head. But that wasn't it at all, as I discovered when the guy opened his mouth wider and wider and then bit down on my cock.

"What the fuck!" I yelled, rising to my feet as I felt a sharp pain rise along my shaft. I couldn't believe it. Nothing like this had ever happened before. Granted, I'd been bobbing my hard, red-G-stringed dick just inches above his open mouth, but he wasn't supposed to put it in his mouth, much less chomp on it with his teeth. I sped down the bar, doing a strategic sidestep sashay around a martini, and jumped down to the floor. I raced through the crowd and up the private set of stairs to the employee restroom. Mikey was there pulsing his rounded pecs in front of the mirror over the sink. I stood beside him and pulled down the front of my G-string, noticing wet teeth marks on the red fabric. I grabbed my dick and searched for broken skin.

"What happened?" Mikey asked, alternately looking at his chest and checking out what I was doing with my dick.

"Some asshole bit my cock," I said.

"Why'd he do that?"

"Fuck if I know," I said, glad to realize I wasn't bleeding. "This place is fucking crazy. I knew I didn't want to work here."

"Want me to kick his ass?" Mikey asked, without turning from his reflection.

"No, that's OK," I answered, a little giddy that he had even asked.

"Well, let me know," he said. "Can't have anybody fucking with The Weapon," he said.

I pulled up my G-string as Danny came running up the stairs saying, "They want you back on the bar. Now!" I rolled my eyes. You'd think having some Jeffrey Dahmer wannabe try to take a bite out of you would get you exempt from the rest of your shift. But no. I dutifully went back downstairs. As I got back on the bar, I told the bartender what happened, but he just laughed it off and offered me a free drink.

"I don't drink," I said.

"What? A dancer that doesn't drink?" he said to the customers around him. "*That's* a new one."

They all laughed.

I moved away and walked right over to Handlebar Mustache Man, who was at the same place on the bar. "Don't you ever fucking do that again," I said to him. He looked up at me and smirked sheepishly. Then he reached into his faded Levi's, grabbed a fistful of bills, and stuffed them all into one of my socks. I took this as an apology.

13

Given how disturbing the cock-biting incident was, I wish I could say that was the last time I worked at Mr. P's, but it wasn't. I danced there several more times until they stopped featuring dancers. I had come to rely on the extra money.

This was just another example of how my personal boundaries weren't as fixed as I once thought they were. I discovered they could stretch like an elastic waistband and give way like a levee.

I realized this again one Saturday night in August when I was working at Secrets and things started out really slow. There was almost nothing worse than being onstage naked and having nobody pay attention to you. You felt futile, pointless, like your existence at this moment in time was a huge mistake. When things were this slow, you were grateful to see the friendly smile of a regular. You'd walk over to the regular and kneel in front of him with gratitude because he's just made your presence matter.

But this night, there were hardly any customers to talk to. I spent most of my time between sets in the dressing room watching Mikey flip through magazines. "Look at this guy," Mikey said, pointing to a Calvin Klein ad featuring Antonio Sabato Jr. in his underwear. "What's he got that I don't have?"

As the night went on, things got even worse. By 11 PM I'd made only $15 in tips. This sucked because I wanted to buy groceries after work. But I had deeper concerns as well. Even though I saw that the night was slow for just about everybody, I worried that it was somehow worse for me. As I danced onstage, idly keeping time to the music, I noticed every time a customer approached another dancer, every time a rolled piece of green paper traveled from a customer's fingers into another dancer's white sock. I'd think, "Where's my tip? Where are my customers?"

A panicked feeling hit me. I began to see the slow night as a sign. I'd been dancing for only a few months, but maybe my career was over. Isn't this the way that sort of thing happens? You start making less and less in tips, and pretty soon you're the pathetic dancer who just shows up for the base pay. Could my time be up already?

"Why's it so fucking slow?" I asked when I got back to the dressing room.

"Slow?" said Mikey. "I'm having a great night. Look what my sugar daddy bought me." He opened up an eyeglass case and pulled out a pair of Ray-Bans.

"Two hundred dollars, baby," he said, putting them on. "Now these are going to take me to the top."

"OK," I said, "let me rephrase. Why is it so slow for everybody but Mikey?"

"It's August," said Danny in the kitchen/dressing room as he changed from a black satin G-string to a blue cotton one. "Everybody's out of town."

This made sense because most of my regulars were missing in action. Not even Michael, my usually reliable dick-on-the-head guy, was there. Dave stopped in, but he left after about thirty minutes to go to La Cage, where Peter was working. Dave was excited about the way things were going with Peter. Recently, Dave had given Peter his phone number so that Peter could keep Dave updated on when and where he was dancing. Peter would call and leave these long stream-of-consciousness messages, and Dave saved them all.

One time when they were talking, Peter told Dave his last name—an act of enormous trust and intimacy within the context of the clubs, where dancers went by first names, most of which were fake. "It was kinda like a break-through," Dave told me.

But still Dave wanted more. "I would like for him to maybe come to my apartment," Dave explained, "even if it wasn't sexual, or maybe we could go to the movies, something like that."

When Dave wasn't at the clubs, he'd daydream about Peter. "I think about being in bed with him all the time," he said. "A lot of times I just think about waking up with him and cuddling with him and having my arm around him or just to be able to go to sleep with my arm around him. That's something I find very arousing.

"It's almost like creative visualization," he continued. "You imagine what you want to happen and it happens. I use creative visualization in all sorts of other areas of my life, and I started thinking, why not use it with this? My inclination with Peter was to always think that something wasn't gonna happen. But then I started thinking, why not omit those negative thoughts and just start thinking of it in a positive way and visualizing it happening? So a lot of times I try to think about the whole thing in detail, like what his reaction would be and what he might say. It's not just sexual. It's the whole trip."

As Dave said this, I thought back to a time when I was at the Follies talking to Peter about having sex with customers.

"Would you ever do it?" I asked while we stood naked, changing in the dressing room.

"For money?"

"Yeah, would you do it for money? Have you?"

"Not much. And not the whole nine yards. I might just, you know, like we'd jerk each other off. But I can't go doing actual intercourse with just anybody."

"Would you ever date a customer?"

"I don't know. I don't want to get too majorly involved with anybody. I just want to, like, entertain."

Based on this conversation, I didn't think Dave's prospects looked too good. But then he told me about something that had happened the last few times he'd seen Peter. For weeks, he'd been telling Peter that he really wanted to see him cum.

"On the bar," Peter exclaimed. "That's totally against the rules!"

"I know, I know," Dave said, trying to calm him. "And I don't want to get you in trouble. But we could do it so no one would know."

Peter, ever the stripping Boy Scout, was totally against the idea at first. There would be no rule-breaking emissions from him, no sirree. But that changed late one Saturday night, when La Cage was nearly empty. Dave sat in the dark, far-left corner of the back bar. The bartender stood clear on the other side doing something with the glasses. Peter moved toward Dave on the bar and kneeled down.

Dave started working on Peter's dick, pulling and stroking, pulling and stroking with his usual studied finesse. Peter threw his head back and moaned.

"How about tonight?" Dave asked.

Peter didn't say anything but he kept letting Dave play with him, pulling and stroking, pulling and stroking. A few more minutes passed, and then Peter moaned again and whispered, "I'm close."

Dave reached for a couple of cocktail napkins with one hand and kept jerking Peter with the other. He looked around. The bartender remained on the far side of the bar, and no other customers or dancers were nearby.

Peter leaned forward with a shake and shot his load into the folded stack of napkins, all the while whispering, "Oh shit. Oh shit. Oh shit."

Hearing Peter swear was almost as unexpected as having him cum on the bar. From then on, Dave began calling what they did together "Oh shit."

"Can we do 'Oh shit' tonight?" he'd ask when he saw Peter.

They started doing it almost every night Dave came in, and Dave even saved the napkins that Peter spunked in.

"Are you serious?" I asked, when he told me this.

"I know it's weird. But they're kind of like mementos. There's a personal experience behind them. If I knew that Peter would pop a load for anybody and everybody, then it wouldn't mean anything to me. But it means something to me because he's told me that I'm the only one he does this with. And I believe him.

"And maybe," he continued, "I keep them because I really like him. I mean, I think I'm . . . I don't know if I should use the word 'love,' but maybe I am a little. Yeah, I mean, I do love him."

"OK, so if he wanted to move in with you, would you let him?"

"He's got it."

"You wouldn't go to the clubs again?"

"He's got it."

When Dave left that night to see Peter, he looked the happiest I'd ever seen him. At least somebody's night was going well.

The only other customer I knew that night was a classical musician from Baltimore, which was about a forty-minute drive away. I'm sure he told me his name a dozen times, but I just thought of him as Symphony Dude. He came to D.C. from time to time, when he was playing a nearby venue, and I always remembered him because he was one of those split-personality-type customers. When I talked with him between sets, we'd converse about film and art and what made him decide to be a musician. But whenever he'd stroke me on the bar, he didn't say much but a bunch of variations on "Your dick is so hot," "That's such a hot dick," and "Your dick is so fucking hot." It wasn't that I wanted him to rhapsodize about Brahms while he was jerking me off, but I would've preferred silence to having my genitals subjected to a barrage of clichés.

I also felt like he wanted me to talk dirty to him and that just wasn't happening. I was fine with a stranger paying a couple of bucks to stroke my cock in public, but adding expletive-laced commentary pushed things past my comfort zone. Still, that night I was grateful to see him. Symphony Dude was always easy to spot. In his early forties, he was younger than most of the customers, and he often wore a stiff white button-down shirt and slacks.

"I just played at the Kennedy Center," he explained when I asked why he was in town.

We talked for a few minutes about the concert, but he seemed a little more anxious than usual. He then abruptly changed the direction of the conversation by saying, "I'll give you fifty bucks if I can watch you cum."

ALL I COULD BARE

The instant he said that, I felt like I'd entered a frozen-in-time moment, one of those occasions when someone says or does something so unexpected that you have no preconceived way to respond. It might seem like I would've gotten these types of requests all the time, and to some extent I did. But usually, customers asked something like, "Do you do private shows?" or "Do you do any work on the side?" To those questions, I had a stock response: "Sorry, I don't do that."

I always said it with a flattered smile, trying hard not to come off as judgmental. I thought of myself almost like a particular model of machine, Boy Stripper X-5000, and my model wasn't equipped to do anything outside the club. Like maybe I hadn't been upgraded with lubricated orifices or my power source stopped working when I was removed from the club.

It's not that I had anything against prostitution. In fact, I'd been obsessed with prostitutes since I was a little boy, riding with my parents down Fourteenth Street, D.C.'s most notorious sex strip in the seventies and eighties. I loved looking at the working girls in their shiny tight outfits, showing off big hair, big shoes, and big attitude. They seemed so tough and unafraid—hands on hips, lips glossy and red, asses switching.

Where other boys wanted to be firemen, baseball players, and astronauts, I wanted to be a sassy, streetwise hooker. I still lament that there were no action figures for boys like me. Imagine my joy upon rushing downstairs on Christmas morning and unwrapping a twelve-inch-tall package containing Lola, the hooker with a heart of gold. I'd dress her up in various polyester and pleather outfits and accessories, and play with her in the optional streetscape playhouse that came complete with a working red light.

Looking back, I think my childhood obsession with prostitutes had to do with how uncomfortable I was with my own burgeoning sexuality. I envied those who seemed so confident about their sexuality that they could stand out on a street corner and sell it. I later learned that my perception was probably far from the reality of the situation. But that's how I felt at the time.

My pro-prostitution attitude stayed with me into adulthood. It didn't make sense that you couldn't sell something that you could give away. It also seemed like prostitution was the wave of the future, because, let's face it, it's now accepted that most love affairs don't last. Why should we be denied sex while we're in between relationships? Wouldn't it be better—and far more efficient, given the time it takes to pick up someone at a bar or even online—to be able to turn to a trusted professional in our sexual time of need?

In some ways, it's even a health issue. Research shows that there are all sorts of benefits associated with sex: increased energy, stress relief, reduction in headaches and joint pain, lower cholesterol levels, weight loss, reduced risk of heart disease, healthier teeth, firmer muscle tone, balanced hormones, and even an enhanced sense of smell. Why should these benefits be limited to those who are lucky enough to be getting some for free? Decriminalizing prostitution would allow us to use money to take care of our sexual yearnings the same way we use it to take care of other basic needs: food, shelter, clothing, spa treatments . . .

But even though I felt strongly about this, I wasn't quite ready to become a full-fledged working boy myself.

I decided to go back into the dressing room and ask Mikey about the private show issue: "Have you ever done one?"

"Sure, I've done them," he said, while doing push-ups on the floor. "But I don't really do them anymore. It kinda fucked me up mentally. I mean, you find yourself doing shit you never imagined you could do."

"So, you strictly keep in the club now?"

"Well, I didn't say that. I mean, I'll still let a guy suck me off. But I want an envelope with at least one hundred bills in it, and I want it in advance."

Well, if Mikey got a hundred bucks for receiving a blow job, then fifty bucks just to spunk off didn't seem so bad. But was cumming for money the same thing as prostitution? The prospect gave new meaning to Cole Porter's "Love for Sale": "love that's fresh and still unspoiled / love that's only slightly soiled." Not to mention "Who would like to sample my supply?"

It was a lot to process. I think when people talk about what they would or wouldn't do for money, they imagine that they'd get an offer and have time to ponder it, consult a few experts, read their horoscope in the morning paper, get a tea leaves reading, and then finally come to a decision. But life doesn't work like that, at least mine didn't while I was stripping. A decision in those circumstances had less to do with the grand scheme of who I thought I was than simply what I needed at the time. And all I was thinking of when he offered to pony up $50 for a spray of my man milk was that this money would allow me to make my regular tip quota, and it would mean that I was still a successful stripper on the come-up and not on my way to becoming a has-been.

"So, how would it work?" I asked him during my next set, leaning closer. He had a clean smell, like bar soap.

"We could go to a booth next door," he said. Next door meant Glorious Health and Amusement, a suck-and-be-sucked porn joint more commonly known as the Glory Hole. I'd never gone there except between sets to buy Certs when my breath was questionable. But I knew enough about the Glory Hole simply from local gay lore.

The place was split into two sides. One side housed a theater—well, actually a stand-up projection screen and some wooden pews—and an elaborate wooden maze that had holes strategically carved within its walls. You could stick your dick through one of the holes and be fully serviced without ever having to deal with something so distracting as a face.

The other side of the Glory Hole, which required separate admission, consisted of aisles of private video booths. You paid a fee to go back there, and then once you were inside your booth, you put tokens in the machine to play your video of choice. This was where Symphony Dude and

I headed after I told him yes. I made this decision mostly because of the $50, but I also didn't feel that what he was asking me to do was all that much of a change from what I did at the club anyway. The only difference was that I got to give myself a happy ending.

As I stood beside Symphony Dude while he paid our admission, I felt like the girlfriend in one of those films set in the fifties, where the guy is paying for a hotel room and the girl is trying her best not to look like the type of girl who would go to a hotel room with a guy she wasn't married to. At least that was my intention, but, of course, demure was hard to pull off wearing shredded jean shorts and a T-shirt that read "Boys, Boys, Boys."

Once he finished paying, we walked toward the video booths, past the plastic-encased walls of porn box covers, the box cover models bearing witness to whatever it was I was doing. It was like I was watching myself in a movie, because my feelings hadn't caught up to my actions. I didn't know how I would feel about jerking off for him or how I would feel afterward. I was as excited to find out what was going to take place as I would've been if I were watching it happen to someone else. Would this incident be liberating for me, the protagonist, or scary? I wanted to know.

We got closer to the booths, and there was a gate, sort of like the turnstile at the entrance of a subway station. The front clerk pushed a button. A sharp buzzing sound went off and the metal bar relaxed to let us through. Then it made a loud click, locking behind us.

There were about a dozen guys standing around in the hallways in front of the booths. They turned when they heard us being buzzed in, but quickly looked away when they saw that Symphony Dude and I were together. I figured that guys must wait back there until they find someone to take into a booth. It was certainly cheaper than paying for a hotel room.

Symphony Dude and I walked past the men. He chose a booth and I followed him in. The space—about the size of a hall coat closet—was hardly big enough for one person, let alone two. There was a stool built into the floor, but if anyone sat on it, there wouldn't be space for the other person. Symphony Dude moved to the back wall and kneeled down. I leaned, as much as I could, against the wall with the built-in video screen. Time was a concern since I was between sets, so I unfastened my jean shorts and let them drop to my ankles. My dick, already rock-hard from the excitement of it all, jutted forward with a heavy bounce. I dug for the Elbow Grease in my sock, dabbed some along my shaft, and began stroking myself. Symphony Dude hurriedly unbuttoned his dress shirt, revealing a plain white T-shirt underneath. "Cum on my chest," he instructed.

Now this request made things feel weird again. I thought: "Why would anyone want me to cum on his shirt? What was he going to do with my cum? Does Spray 'n Wash work on cum stains?"

These thoughts began distracting me, so I tried to keep them out of my mind. As I kept jerking, he used the tips of his fingers to softly stroke my inner thighs and launched into his mantra: "Oh, your dick is so hot," "That is one hot dick," "Your dick is so fucking hot."

After what seemed like about five minutes, I asked when he wanted me to cum. "Whenever you're ready," he said, opening up his shirt even wider. I saw some gray-flecked chest hair peek out from around his collar. I started stroking faster and closed my eyes. I wasn't really turned on, but I wasn't exactly turned off, either. Jerking off this time was just something I was doing to provoke a physical response, like sticking my finger down my throat in order to throw up. I jerked faster. I felt myself start to sweat a little under my arms, around my hairline, and beneath my balls. More jerking. Pulling on my cock and holding my balls from underneath. Then came that tingly, rising sensation that starts somewhere around my knees. I was close.

"Here goes," I said, before splattering his undershirt with a slew of cloudy white splotches.

"Oh, fuck yeah," he moaned, although I don't believe he came himself. His pants were still buttoned and he wasn't even touching his cock. (Or at least that's how I remember it. Thinking back, it seems weird that he wouldn't have gotten himself off. I wonder if I don't recall him cumming because it feels safer, more like I was giving a command performance and not engaging in a bout of mutual masturbation, which would make it more like sex. I honestly don't know what the truth of the matter is.)

As soon as I came, I felt uncomfortable. What should I do or say next? I pulled up my shorts. "That was really fun," I said flatly. He rose up from his knees, buttoned his shirt, and started fumbling for money in his right pocket. Out came two twenty-dollar bills and a ten, which he handed to me. Both of us were looking down.

I reached for the money and as I touched the dry bills, part of me expected the walls to fall down, colored lights to flash, and sirens to wail, as a posse of the police, my mother and father, assorted family members, and maybe an elementary school teacher or two stared at me in shame.

But alas, nothing happened.

I followed Symphony Dude out of the booth, through the aisles, past the shining box covers, and back to the dark street.

"Are you coming back inside?" I asked him at the door to Secrets.

"No, I'm gonna head home. That was fun, though. Thanks."

I noticed that he had buttoned up his shirt, although it was still untucked. I felt like saying, "Dude, I can't believe you're going to drive all the way back to Baltimore with my spunk on your chest." I felt bad, like I should offer him a wet wipe or something. It was all too weird, and the weirdest part of it was that he was the one with cum all over him but I felt uncomfortable.

It made me realize that part of being an effective sex worker was having a nonjudgmental attitude about other people's desires. I once met this beefy straight Midwestern frat-boy-turned-gay-porn-star-turned-escort who told me about this one customer of his who owned a specially designed chair that was like a potty training seat. The trick would lie underneath the chair, which was raised off the ground on legs, and Frat Boy would sit on the seat and take a dump right on the trick's face. When Frat Boy told me about this, I felt my insides squeeze up. But he relayed this detail as if he was a bartender telling me about a customer who liked an extra slice of lemon in his cosmo. Frat Boy could shit on somebody's face without reservation, yet I felt strange about cumming on someone's shirt. I realized that I'd never make a good working boy, and I couldn't help but feel a little disappointed. A boyhood dream deferred.

14

Prostitution wasn't my only sex-for-cash–related obsession, though. Ever since I've known that there were guys who get paid to fuck on camera, I've wanted to be one of those lucky Joes or Jons or Dillons or Mavericks. I think I was fascinated with porn stars for the same reason I was attracted to prostitutes. They seemed sexually powerful to me and I was hungry to know how that felt. One fringe benefit of stripping was that I got to meet a lot of porn stars who came to town to dance. I had the opportunity to examine them closely in the dressing room—and see if the camera adds inches as well as pounds. I also got to ask them all of my burning questions about the biz.

My understanding of what it meant to be a porn star had changed so much since I started dancing. I remembered when I saw Joey Stefano at La Cage all those years ago.

I imagined that he swept into town on a first-class flight, possibly chartered, and was whisked in a limo from the airport to his luxury penthouse suite at the Watergate. The limo waited for him as he prepared for his performance—a ritual that, in my mind, involved yoga, a personal masseuse, and a bath of lavender-scented Evian—and then took him to the club, with the limo driver talking to him all the while to distract Joey from noticing the crummy neighborhood. But I soon discovered that the touring life for most porn stars is a far more Greyhound bus/Southwest Airlines/Days Inn affair.

(Also, Joey's drug-overdose death in 1994 showed me that porn definitely had a dark side.)

One Sunday, I worked at the Follies with an up-and-coming porn star, Clay Maverick. I hadn't even heard of him before, but when I met him, I almost had the wind knocked out of me. He had the lean chiseled body of a hot Greek statue, and the face of someone you might cast as Superman. If I had known he was so amazing looking, I would've gone to the video store and done some research.

After the noon set, I was on my way out to grab some lunch when I noticed him sitting idly in the lobby. Some golf game was flickering on the TV.

"Hey, do you need a ride somewhere?"

"Yeah," he said. "It'd be great if you could give me a ride back to my hotel. I don't want to waste money on a cab."

"Sure," I said. "I'm also going to grab something to eat and you're welcome to join me."

"Cool," he said.

As I was talking to him, the whole scene felt surreal. Here I was, this geeky grad student, giving a genuine porn star a ride to his hotel and inviting him to lunch. How weird was this?

We got in my red Neon—Seth and I had bought it about a year before—and started on our way. I instantly became obsessed with his comfort, like I was his personal flight—or in this case, car—attendant.

"Are you cold, or hot?" I asked, fiddling with the controls. "Would you like the radio on, or off? What kind of music do you like?"

If I'd had pillows and a blanket in the backseat, I would have surely offered them to him.

"I'm cool," he kept saying, which after the fifth or sixth time I took as code for "Dude, leave me alone."

We decided to eat at the Boston Chicken in Dupont Circle, because he was attempting to get in as many calories as he could.

"I'm trying for three to four thousand each day," he said. "I'm still too lean. I want to get bigger."

With that revelation I knew Clay was straight. I couldn't imagine any gay guys describing themselves as "too lean," whereas, on the other hand, all the straight dancers I knew were obsessed with getting bigger and bulkier. The gay body ideal was Spider-Man; the straight aesthetic leaned to Thor.

We ordered our food—him, two servings of the meat loaf platter; me, a couple of vegetable sides—and then sat down in the upstairs dining area that overlooked Connecticut Avenue.

"So, what do you make of the Follies?" I asked.

"I don't know. It left a bad taste in my mouth," he said, forking a sauce-covered hunk of meat loaf. "The way the customers treat you is kind of degrading. They treat you like a whore, pretty much. I mean, they think they can do anything to you and touch you everywhere. It's like a free-for-all, and you've got to really throw down to get them off you. So I doubt I'll ever do it again after this time. I think I'm just going to stick to doing movies."

"How'd you start doing those?"

"Well, I started out dancing back in Seattle a couple of years ago when I was in high school . . ."

"Wait a minute. How old are you?"

"I'm almost twenty-one."

"Wow, you're a baby." His age surprised me. I was twenty-seven and had a hard time believing that anybody interesting could be younger than me.

"So anyway, when I was in high school I was dating this stripper for a long while and she kept trying to get me to dance at this straight club. She told me I could make a lot of money and she was like, 'If you don't like it, you don't have to do it.' So one night—it was this total spur-of-the-moment thing—I just went there and said, 'Hey, I want to dance,' and they let me audition.

"I sucked at first," he continued, "because all the dancers there were like Chippendales'. But they let me dance because of my body, and I just kept on doing it and doing it until I got better and better. I would peep the really good dancers and watch them. It's all about your moves, the body, the way you dance, your attitude, how you handle yourself, everything."

"So how'd this lead to porn?"

"Well, I started working at this gay place because I had a blowout with the boss at the other club. He called my girlfriend a bitch and I told him to, you know, pretty much fuck off."

"Was it harder to dance for men, or women?"

"I don't know. Women are good looking, but they make you put on a show and work harder. With guys, you just stand there and move around a little bit.

"I became very popular at the gay place," he said, adding that one of his best customers was an actor who played the portly father on a black family sitcom, "and one day this porn guy came into the club and gave me his card. I threw it away the first time. But he came in another time, gave me his card again, and I decided to give him a call. We talked and the next day he flew me and my girlfriend to L.A. for me to do this gay scene. I asked about straight porn but he said guys get paid more for gay stuff."

"What movie was this for?"

"I don't know. They don't tell you that. Or if they did, I don't remember. I never pay attention. You just do a scene and they put it in a movie somewhere."

"So I'm guessing this was the first time you'd ever done it with a guy."

"Oh yeah."

"So how'd it go?"

"How'd it go?"

"Yeah, I mean, was it cool, gross, what?"

"I was more trying to concentrate on how to do it 'cause I didn't know how, you know, it worked. They had to explain it to me pretty much, like the kind of positions and, you know, how to stick it in without hurting the guy and stuff."

"And your girlfriend was with you the whole time?"

"Yeah, laughing her ass off. She thought the whole thing was hilarious, like they had to teach me how to fuck. I told her that with guys it's different."

"Did you have dialogue and stuff?"

"Yeah, a little. But I try to avoid dialogue. Dialogue's not a good thing. I can't act. I just try to play it off."

"Do you watch your films?"

"No, I can't do it."

"But you like making them?"

"I just want it to lead to as much money as I can get out of it," he said, using a roll to sop up the remaining sauce on his otherwise empty plate. "Then in about two years I want to open up my own business, like a strip club but more of a show club. You know, like a high-class place with shows and stuff."

Later, after I'd dropped him off at his hotel, I kept thinking about his observations on the porn business. He made it seem a lot more laid-back and performer-friendly than I'd imagined. I could see myself on a set, exchanging laughs with cast and crew while an adorable straight guy got first-hand—or first *dick*—instruction in butt sex. It made me want to try it out, and one night I got my shot.

It happened one Saturday, when I was having a particularly sucky night: it was slow; I wasn't making any money; and on top of it, I felt fat because I ate a pizza before work.

It was always a horrible feeling to be bloated and naked in front of strangers. For some reason, it made me feel *more* naked. Like I was a Thanksgiving float that someone forgot to clothe.

By this point I'd been dancing for several months and I'd recently made a move from Secrets to Wet, a newer club that drew a younger, trendier crowd. As a dancer, it was important to move around from club to club because you always made more money when you were a new face.

In addition to featuring a shower at the back of the bar, Wet also had the reputation for being a local porn star launching pad. Scouts from L.A. often visited the club looking for new talent. And they even used the club to film the porn video *Striptease*.

I was on my second-to-last set, dying to go home, when this short blond guy walked over to where I was dancing on the bar (I'd since gotten over my dancing-on-the-bar phobia) and tipped me a five-dollar bill. It was kind of a shock, because I hadn't been tipped that whole set. I knelt down.

"Thanks a lot," I said. "How are you?"

"Great now," he answered, grabbing hold of my jewels.

"I don't think I've seen you here before."

"No, I've been here before. But I'm in town this time with Chi Chi LaRue. Have you ever heard of her?"

"Sure," I said. Chi Chi LaRue was a notorious drag

queen/porn director who unapologetically called her films "fuck flicks."

"Well, I'm a talent scout for her and some other directors."

"Cool."

"Have you ever thought about doing porn?"

Had I thought about it? Most guys I knew—in and out of the biz—had *thought* about it.

"I guess so," I said.

"I'd love if you'd audition for me," he said, tipping me another $5 and softly rubbing my calf. "You could be a star."

"You think so?"

"Yeah. You've got a cute face, nice body, nice dick. I can totally see it."

"What would I need to do to audition?"

"I'd just need to get a Polaroid of you to take back to L.A."

Hmm, I thought. That seemed reasonable. But I really wasn't in a making-major-life-decisions kind of mood. I was tired, cranky, and feeling blubbery.

"I'll think about it," I said.

"OK," he answered, slipping me another $5 before I got up and moved down the bar.

After my set was over, I went back to the dressing room and mulled the porn idea over. What was I so afraid of? He just wanted to take my picture. I still had plenty of time to think it over before I actually *made* a video, if I wanted to make one. Did I want to make one? I thought so. Maybe? But was this something that I really wanted to do, like as the real me? Or was it as fantasy, something an alternative version of me would do? A muscled, oiled-up porn me. I couldn't quite figure it out.

When it was time for my next set, I walked back on the bar and saw that Porn Guy was one of the only customers left at the club.

"So, you're not going to let me take your picture," he said when I walked over to him.

"I don't know," I said, bending down to talk with him. "I'm not really up to it tonight."

"It's no big deal," he said, tipping me another $5. "I'll only use the picture to see if any directors are interested in you."

"Maybe another night. Are you going to be around tomorrow?"

"No, this is my last day in town."

"Sorry," I said, shrugging my shoulders.

I moved away and spent the rest of the set gossiping with two of the other dancers at the back of the bar. When the set was over, I dashed back into the dressing room, threw on my jeans and a T-shirt, grabbed my duffel bag, and started out the door. Porn Guy nodded and waved at me as I left.

I got in the Neon and started driving away. But as I made it to the first stoplight, I started thinking, "What do I have to lose?" It wasn't like he was asking me to make a porno right then and there. What if this was my only chance to try something like this? Was I being smart by walking away, or did this signal the return of Wimpy Craig, the guy who doesn't do the things he dreams about, the guy who studies things as opposed to lives them?

I turned the car around. I still wasn't sure if I actually wanted to make a porn video, but I figured it wouldn't hurt to find out if I *could*. I walked back in the club and told Porn Guy that he could take my picture.

"Great," he said enthusiastically. "The only thing is my camera is back at my hotel. We'll have to go there to take the picture."

This struck me as a little weird; and in retrospect, it should have set off alarm bells. But at the time it made sense that he wouldn't have his camera with him. What kind of geek goes clubbing with a big Polaroid swinging around his neck?

We left the club, jumped in my car, and drove to a Best Western a couple of blocks away. The hotel was officially called the Best Western Capitol Skyline, because it offered a grand view of the U.S. Capitol dome—that is, if you could look past the Wendy's, the McDonald's, and the Exxon in the foreground. A lighted sign in front of the Best Western touted the "Friday Night Fish Fry in the Skyline Lounge."

As I walked to his room, down the long dark hallway covered with patterned seventies-looking wallpaper, I felt the same way as I did when going to the Glory Hole with Symphony Guy. It was like I was playing "me" in a film. Yet, at the same time, I knew that my quickening heartbeat and the sweat seeping from my armpits were not put-ons. The moment at once was unreal and all too real.

We got to his room and he asked me to strip to my undies. "Tightie whities," he observed. "Nice." It was all a part of my boy-next-door look.

He took a couple of shots of me in my underwear standing against the wall, which featured more geometric wall patterns, this time in gleaming gold.

"Uh, could you suck your gut in a little bit?" he asked.

I did, or at least I thought I did.

"A little more," he said.

"Damn, why did I eat all of that pizza?" I screamed in my head.

"OK, now take off your underwear."

Not a problem, I thought. I felt comfortable with this part of the photo shoot. I knew that once I dropped my drawers, ol' reliable would immediately stand at attention.

"You have a really nice dick," he said.

"Thanks," I answered proudly.

But then the trouble started. He told me to grab my cock so that it stood straight up. But he said I could use only two fingers so my hand wouldn't cover my dick. Some guys must find this easy to do because porn models have to do it all the time when they take pictures. But for me, it was like advanced yoga. We tried it for several minutes, and I just couldn't get it right. My dick kept slipping from my grasp just as he snapped the picture.

He sighed and then said, somewhat exasperated, "Let me just get a shot of your asshole."

"OK," I said, feeling frustrated and ready to leave. "What do you need me to do?"

"Get on the bed and bend over on all fours."

I climbed atop the shiny bedspread and assumed my best doggy-style position. I heard a click and the slide of the Polaroid film coming from the camera.

"Wait a minute," he said. I heard him walk into the bathroom and then come back out. Suddenly, I felt some cold, slimy goop sliding down my ass crack.

"What the fuck is that?" I asked, whipping my head around.

"Oh," he said. "I wanted to put some lotion on your asshole to make it shinier."

"Fuck," I thought as I turned back around, "this is all getting too weird." It felt like I was about to get my ass plowed by the turdlike green thing from *Ghost Busters*— I'd been slimed!

"This is good," he said, as I felt a finger poke around in my cheeks, smoothing out my ass hair.

I heard several more clicks, more film sliding from the camera. "How many pictures of a greased-up asshole can you possibly need?" I thought.

"OK, now flip over," he said. I rolled over and slid down the bedspread.

"Do you cum a lot?" he asked.

"Depends, I guess."

"It would be really good if we could see you cum."

"OK," I said thinking that, after having an ass full of Best Western lotion, popping a load wasn't going to be any more humiliating. I really just wanted to get out of there. But I figured that I had to see it through.

I lay down on my back, closed my eyes, and started jerking, trying to get the job done as quickly as possible. Then I felt the bed move. I opened my eyes and saw that Porn Guy had put down his camera and was now unzipping his own pants.

"Your dick is really turning me on," he said, grabbing hold of his own stubby penis. He started jerking himself off, faster and faster, making the whole bed shake. I closed my eyes again and conjured up the hottest ass I could imagine. I came quickly, not much, but at least I was done. A few seconds later, Porn Guy cried out, "Oh, yes," and sprayed all over the bedspread next to me.

I jumped up and went into the bathroom, spotting the open tube of hotel lotion by the sink. I grabbed a clean towel and wiped myself off. Then I looked in the mirror, looked closely at my face, into my eyes. It was still the same face I saw each and every morning. Everything was still the same. I balled up the towel in my hand and threw it on the floor.

"Thanks for coming by," Porn Guy said as I walked out of the bathroom and started putting on my clothes. "I'll call you if anything comes of the pictures."

"All right," I said, heading toward the door.

"Maybe I'll see you the next time I come to town with Chi Chi," he said.

"Yeah, see you," I said, with the door closing behind me. As I made my thirty-minute ride home, I felt lotion swishing around in my buns whenever I shifted my weight or made a turn. I felt like Irene Cara when she auditioned for that pervert in *Fame*. It was my bare-titty moment. I drove along and the lyrics to Cara's "Out Here on My Own" played in my head: "We're always provin' who we are / Always reachin' for the rising star." I wondered why I had ultimately decided to go back to the hotel with Porn Guy; why hadn't I just said no? I also wondered if he would call.

15

One evening in July, I arrived for work at Wet and saw something shocking, like a giant cock falling from the sky. There was a sign on the back of the dressing room door that read: "Attention All Dancers: You are not to be touched, fondled, fingered, or stroked in any shape, form, or fashion. This applies both to customers and yourselves. Your cooperation is both expected and appreciated. Thank you, Management."

"Not to be touched, fondled, fingered, or stroked," I said to the other dancers in the room. "What are we supposed to do—*dance*?"

"Yeah, and we can't even touch ourselves," said Jay, a new dancer I'd met at Wet who was slipping into his stiff white sailor pants.

"I know, why bother?" said another dancer, a blond from the Virginia sticks. "It wasn't even worth the drive to come here."

"Does anybody know why?" I asked.

"Something about the alcohol board cracking down on the strip clubs," Jay said, before walking out onto the bar.

I followed him out, wearing my jean shorts, a G-string, and a T-shirt. I felt overdressed since I usually went out commando in a pair of jean shorts, but I didn't want to risk any dick exposure until I found out what was going on.

I asked the bartender what was up and he gave me the scoop. Apparently some inspectors from the D.C. Alcoholic Beverage Control Board visited the club a few months before and saw dancers playing with themselves and customers playing with dancers—in other words, what happened at Wet and the other strip clubs every night and had been for years. But where the alcohol board had once turned a blind eye to the clubs, it now appeared to be cracking down, since it was technically illegal for sexual acts—however defined—to take place in establishments serving alcohol. And these were serious charges. Wet faced a ten-thousand-dollar fine and permanent revocation of its liquor license.

For this reason, the club wasn't playing when it came to enforcing the new rules. Some of the club's security guards were recommissioned as monitors to watch what was going on between the customers and the dancers.

"And anyone who breaks the rules," the bartender told me, "will be fired immediately."

Hmm, I thought to myself, nothing like the threat of losing your job to put you in the mood to get nekkid and sexy. But nevertheless, I put on a brave face as I took off my jeans and began to remove my G-string. I tried to take my time with this because I knew my cock was in foxhole mode, staying as close to my body as possible like a scared kid to his mother's breast. The conditions in the club worked to produce maximal shrinkage. Not only was there all this tension in the air, but it was as if the Coldmeister himself was working the air-conditioning, villainously turning it up so that we couldn't get our boy batons to stand at attention. I tried to move my G-string around to create some heating friction, but to no avail. Finally, I just took it off to reveal that I had a sad and sickly snail hanging between my legs.

I walked over to Michael, who had started coming to Wet once he found out I was working there. He was seated by himself at the bar, studying the ice cubes in his drink more closely than ever before. He put two bucks in my sock and I tried to sort of wiggle my limp cock around for him. But he just laughed, and I threw my hands up like "What can I do?" There would be no head-banging cock action tonight.

Michael, at least, had a sense of humor about what was going on. Most of the other customers were pissed as they now had to deal with signs telling them not to touch, obtrusive security guards watching their every move, and their hands getting slapped by dancers when they crossed one of the newly drawn lines. In one night, Wet went from a relaxed, good-time free-for-all to a strict kindergarten class with pricey drinks and a cover charge. Not surprisingly, attendance plummeted.

By the next night, we were dancing for only about three or four guys at a time. They'd come in, figure out what was going on, and quickly abandon us for La Cage or Secrets, which were still, at least temporarily, in business-as-usual mode. Frustration built among the dancers and management, which let us sneak a few grabs and touches over the weekend because we weren't making any money. But by the next week, a new sign appeared on the back of the dressing room door: "Sorry, Guys. We are back to no touching by the customers and you can't touch yourself or another dancer! Sorry & thanks." Apparently, someone got wind that the ABC investigators might come back.

That night, I tried to stay in a good frame of mind, since for the past few weeks I'd been feeling like Grumpy Stripper Smurf, which was never a good attitude for getting tips. I thought I'd even try to dance a little, as I started to do a more purposeful take on my side-to-side two-step and even threw in some ass wiggles and dramatic *Flashdance*-like head jerks. But I was bored by the end of the first song, a dance mix of Toni Braxton's "You're Makin' Me High" that seemed like it was never gonna end.

It was too late in the game for me to try to be Jennifer Beals or, for that matter, her dancing stunt double, Marine Jahan. I spent the rest of the night wandering from one part of the bar to the other like some kind of flaccid nude loiterer. I knew something had to give.

One of the songs the D.J. played that night was a Wet staple, "Movin' On," a minor club hit by the British girl group Bananarama. (In the eighties, I was a big fan and would work myself into a closeted-gay-boy frenzy over "Doctor Love," "Robert De Niro's Waiting," "I Heard a Rumor," and "Some Girls." But after the group lost my favorite member, Siobhan, I'd stopped caring.) I'd heard the song dozens of times, but I'd never paid attention to the lyrics, happily occupied as I was with hands on my dick and money in my sock. But that night the downsized divas seemed to be chirping right to me: "I know we planned to stay together / We just ran into stormy weather."

I had thought about quitting Wet as I drove in that night, but now I decided I was really going to leave. With the new rules in place, I wasn't making any money and it wasn't any fun. People assumed that I'd prefer not being touched—and a lot of dancers did—but I always liked that aspect of dancing once I got used to it. And it wasn't just because I was lazy and, unlike Donna Summer, didn't want to work too hard for the money. I enjoyed the weird intimacy of the touching, how it created this hard-to-define physical connection between two virtual strangers, a dialogue of flesh on flesh. I wasn't just a detached fantasy figure for the customers. I was warm and could respond to their touch. This made it more exciting than just dancing around being gawked at. And did I mention the whole lazy thing?

At the end of the night, I told the manager not to put me on the schedule for the following week, that I wouldn't be back. He halfheartedly tried to talk me out of it, telling me that things were gonna get better. But I could tell he didn't believe it himself. (In fact, things got a whole lot worse for the club in the short run. The ABC Board fined Wet $10,000 and suspended its liquor license, forcing it to close for several weeks.)

As I drove home that night, I had the chorus of that Bananarama song stuck in my head: " . . . I don't know where I'm going / But I'm movin' on." It was one of those moments when the silliest pop song can seem profound for the way it nails what you're going through. The truth was that I didn't know where the fuck I was going.

I had done the stripping thing and had been relatively unscathed, save for some creepy moments and the whole slippery-ass-crack porn-audition fiasco. (Porn Guy never called, by the way.) I hadn't become part of a big University of Maryland sex scandal; and my parents were still blissfully in the dark about what their only begotten son was doing in the dark.

Also, things were still going well in my relationship with Seth. We were now going on six years. Sometimes we'd be sitting on our couch together watching an episode of *Buffy the Vampire Slayer* or *The X-Files* that he'd taped for me while I was at work, and I'd think, "This is what it must feel like to last."

But despite these good things, I didn't know what it all meant, how it added up. Stripping had been a fun experience, but I wasn't any closer to resolving the issues that had led me to strip in the first place. The only thing I knew was that it had nothing to do with academic research anymore. It was totally personal, even if I couldn't articulate how.

My head was filled with questions as I pulled into the parking lot at my apartment complex and saw that the living room light was on, indicating that Seth was probably waiting up for me. All I was certain about was what Bananarama had been singing: "I'm movin' on."

16

A few weeks after leaving Wet, I was sitting in the Follies, where I continued to work while I figured out what I wanted to do with my life. I could've tried going back to Secrets or getting a job at La Cage. But all the clubs were now strictly "no touch" since in the weeks following the bust at Wet, ABC investigators also cited La Cage for allowing dancers to "perform or simulate acts of masturbation" and for letting "customers and entertainers . . . fondle in an erotic manner the genitals of another person." The local gay press reported these charges as "allegations," which was like saying the sky is allegedly blue and that the Declaration of Independence states that all men are, allegedly, created equal.

It appeared that the clubs were now part of a full-scale crackdown, and no one could figure out why this was happening after decades when they were left alone. Conspiracy theories abounded—somebody wasn't paid off; the head of the ABC was a homophobe. Even the mayor's office seemed perplexed by the charges. Members of Marion Barry's gay community advisory committee criticized the ABC for "overpenalizing" gay bars. The protection Barry had once offered the gay community had faded along with his credibility since his January 1990 arrest for using crack cocaine in a hotel room with an ex-girlfriend. The whole thing was caught on tape, including Barry notoriously muttering, "Bitch set me up . . . I shouldn't have come up here . . . Goddamn bitch," as F.B.I. agents put him in hand-cuffs.

Barry ultimately spent six months in jail after being convicted of misdemeanor cocaine possession, a situation that also cost him his position as mayor. He rebounded a couple of years later, first by winning a D.C. council seat in 1992 and two years later, in a stunning turn of events, being elected mayor again. But by this time the role of a D.C. mayor had changed dramatically. A financial control board now oversaw city contracts, programs, and many other things that were formerly the purview of the mayor. The once powerful Barry was now essentially a figurehead, so he was in no position to take on the Alcoholic Beverage Control Board.

Regular customers had a hard time accepting the changes and they stopped coming in droves. They would even chat about it on website message boards, referring to the new no-touch regulations collectively as "The Rule." One guy posted that he was "so frustrated" that he was turning to escorts to satisfy his "appetite for young dudes." Another wrote: "I am dismayed to hear that 'The Rule' is still in effect. What a shame! I live about three hours away and used to get up to D.C. monthly. It just doesn't seem worth the drive when touching is not permitted. Can't someone be bribed or something? Why after so many years has D.C. gone conservative? Please give me an update if the situation changes." It was the end of an era, but no one was ready to accept it.

For dancers, The Rule translated into a dramatic dip in tips. The only place that wasn't affected was the Follies. Because it didn't serve liquor, it wasn't under the ABC Board's control. Things were as touchy-feely as always, and it became increasingly popular since it was the only hands-on game in town. The only problem for me was that the Follies featured dancers only on the weekend and the management liked to keep the dancer lineup changing. The most I could work there was about two to three days a month—not exactly enough to keep the rent paid and the lights on.

This all happened at an especially bad time because I had also made the decision to take a leave from grad school and give up my teaching assistantship, which was my only other form of income. I'd enjoyed my summer outside the ivory tower, talking to regular folks about regular things—TV, music, sex—without having to dissect them, abstract them, or run them through some theoretical grinder. I needed to figure out who I wanted to be in the world, a question that all my years in school had allowed me to avoid.

Emotionally, Seth tried to understand what I was going

through, but I could tell he just didn't get it. He lived for class preparation, pontificating on the latest literary theories, and putting on tweed jackets to deliver conference papers before rapt audiences of three to five people. I knew it was hard for him to grasp why I no longer wanted that life, if I ever had truly wanted it at all.

His patience was particularly tested now that I was bringing in less cash. We had to cut luxuries like our weekly Ethiopian dinner and seeing movies at night instead of during budget matinees. In order to pick up some of the financial slack, Seth took on additional classes so that he was now teaching English full time at the University of Maryland and at a local art college. Then, on his off day, Friday, he would sometimes do office temp work when things were really tight. Seth was a speed demon on the keyboard so he was always in demand at the temp agency. I also tried to do temp work, but after I took the typing test, the agency rep drolly asked me if I had any experience answering phones. Not surprisingly, I didn't get any work.

The guilt I felt about Seth working more than me, predictably, made me act like an asshole. As I sat at home obsessing over the most minute plot points of *The Young and the Restless,* I would call him on his cell phone constantly to break news about, say, what we got in the mail that day ("You wouldn't believe the amount of junk") or to ask what time he would be home (it was pretty much the same time each day), and what *he* planned to make for dinner. Then, if for some reason he didn't answer, I'd leave emergency messages asking him to stop and pick up some

Diet Coke on the way home or to tell him about a really cool song that I'd just heard on the radio. These calls had the effect of not only being annoying but also running up our cell phone bill, which put us further in the hole. But when Seth complained, I sniped that all we ever talked about was money. The bizarre thing was that I knew I was acting like an ass, but I couldn't stop myself. It was like someone else was scripting my lines and I wasn't a big enough star to demand a rewrite.

Feeling desperate, I started thinking about testing the sex-for-money waters again. Yes, my previous attempts—with Symphony Dude and Porn Dude—had been awful and awkward. But now I was a little bit older and possibly even wiser, not to mention a lot more desperate. Without telling Seth, I made an appointment for an interview with an escort agency that advertised in the back of the local gay newspaper.

The place was located in the basement of a brownstone near Dupont Circle. When I got there, I pushed the door-bell and a balding heavyset white guy, the owner, came to the door. He told me that he was starving and asked if I wouldn't mind joining him for dinner at a nearby restaurant. "No problem," I told him. I even wondered if this was some kind of test to see if I could actually pull off the escorting part of being an escort.

As we walked to the restaurant, I tried to pin him down about what was actually expected of his working boys, but he kept being vague, saying things like "It depends on the customer" or "Whatever the guy on the call is comfortable with." He made it sound like it wasn't all that different from what I'd already been doing. But I figured that it couldn't really be *that* easy, so over a fried calamari appetizer, I decided to be direct.

"So, you don't have to get fucked or anything, do you?" I asked.

Although I was a lot more comfortable with taking it up the ass than I had been when I first came out, I still thought of it more as an interruption of regularly scheduled programming, or like something to barter with, say, when I wanted to get out of doing the dishes or taking out the trash. I definitely didn't want it written into my regular job description.

"No," he assured me. "If that's your thing, then you can make a lot of money doing it. But you don't have to."

"Yeah, I see myself pretty exclusively as a top," I said, "professionally speaking."

He nodded.

"Do a lot of the customers want to be fucked?" I asked.

I figured I could pretty much stick my dick in anything, especially if my dong was sheathed in plastic, although the thought of dealing with any flesh—hairy, flabby, bumpy, or sweaty—in the way of the targeted orifice might gross me out.

"No," he said, "most of the clients don't even want that."

"So what are they looking for?" I asked, figuring it couldn't all be candlelit dinners and conversation like in those hooker-with-a-heart-of-gold movies.

"Blow jobs, mainly," he said. "They're mostly looking for oral."

"Oh, do you have to, like, give *and* receive?"

"Well," he said, chewing on a piece of bread, "I don't think anybody is going to pay to give a blow job and not expect something in return."

"Oh," I repeated. I wasn't sure what else to say. I knew instantly that this wasn't the right job for me. There were a lot of sexual things that I could imagine doing for money, but diving face-first into some stranger's funky rain forest of pubes was not one of them.

I guessed things had changed since the sixties, back when John Rechy wrote his hustler opus *City of Night* and a working boy could make a decent living just by letting some troll toke on his johnson. But alas, the gay liberation movement had raised expectations all around and reciprocating was now the way of the day. This was just more proof that the stud-for-hire thing would never be for me. I thanked the escorting don for his time—*and the grilled salmon dinner*—but I told him that I didn't think I could get with sucking a lot of strange dicks. I mean, I don't even drink after my parents. Fortunately, he seemed to understand. Cold feet were probably common in his business.

We parted ways and as I walked back to my car, I couldn't help but be disappointed that I was no closer to solving my money problems. I immediately called home and asked Seth what he had cooked for dinner, even though I'd just eaten.

17

The only thing giving me hope during this time was a vague idea that I might someday want to be a writer—not a person who places dense articles in obscure academic journals, but somebody who really has a voice in the world. I used to think about being a writer when I was in elementary school and junior high, but I thought the dream had faded. Really, it had just gone underground like a sleeper agent waiting to suicide-bomb my priorities.

The idea of becoming a writer slowly came to dominate my thinking. I started sitting with a pile of newspapers and magazines during my breaks at the Follies. I studied them, getting to know different writers and learning each publication's tone and style. At first, I thought I was too old to try to break into this kind of writing. But then I read somewhere that one of my favorite writers, former

New Yorker film critic Pauline Kael, didn't pen her first review until she was around thirty-five. Hell, I wasn't even thirty.

But even while I nurtured this dream of becoming a writer, I had the more pressing problem of trying to make a living in the here and now. Fortunately, one day while flipping through the employment section of the local gay newspaper, I found—amid numerous listings for bartenders and nude house cleaners—an ad for educator/coordinator of the Male Sex Industry Project at D.C.'s Whitman-Walker Clinic, one of the most respected AIDS organizations in the country. This seemed right up my alley—I was already an educator and I certainly had my share of experiences working in the male sex industry.

I wrote a letter to the human resources director detailing my teaching background as well as my experience studying the male sex industry, focusing on what I called "the social function of stripping." "I have also worked as a stripper in order to get an inside view of the issues male strippers face," I wrote. This approach apparently was effective. About a week after sending the letter, I was downtown at the clinic for an interview.

Things went well as I met with the woman who would be my boss. She explained that the job entailed distributing condoms at local night spots and sex clubs and trying to establish and run educational programs for male sex workers and gay men in general. As we talked, I pretty much felt I was a shoo-in for the job, until my last appointment of the day, a meeting with one of the clinic's top administrators.

This guy had been with the clinic since the early eighties when AIDS was still a relatively uncharted mystery, and he had become a local gay hero.

I felt a little intimidated as he welcomed me into his office with the hurried demeanor of someone with a lot on his plate. The room, which was dark and wooden, made me feel like a naughty English schoolboy who'd been sent to the headmaster's office for hitting a classmate in the balls with a cricket stick.

"I read in your letter that you used to work as a stripper," the administrator said, as I lowered myself with a *thunk* on his stiff leather sofa.

"Yes," I answered in my most polished interview voice. "I studied the clubs as a part of my graduate work. I thought it was important to understand the phenomenon from a firsthand perspective."

"What did you find out?" he asked, shuffling through some papers in his hand.

"Well, it's complicated," I said. "I guess a lot of people think that the whole scene is about horny old guys being worked over by a bunch of money-hungry hustlers. But I found out that it's often much more than that."

"And you're done with stripping now?"

"Yes," I said, and it technically wasn't a lie. True, I'd worked at the Follies just the previous weekend, but I didn't have any additional dates scheduled.

"You also wrote something about the 'social function' of

stripping," he said in the way that someone might cry out, "What stinks?"

This made me nervous. I didn't want to blow getting the job.

"Um," I started, "what I meant is that the clubs serve the social function of bringing together diverse groups of men—openly gay, closeted, straight, young, old, black, white, et cetera—in ways that they wouldn't likely interact otherwise. And I guess that's partly why I find the whole scene interesting."

"I have to tell you," he said, finally looking up from his papers, "we're not at all interested here in the social function of stripping or anything else. We're trying to save lives."

"Of course," I said. "I understand that. Although I think that in order to reach people with any kind of message, you have to first understand where they're coming from."

"Oh, I understand where they're coming from. From my experience, most of them are prostitutes and drug addicts and the best thing we can do is try to stop them from spreading the virus."

"Well, that might be your experience, but it certainly isn't mine," I said, the tone of my voice noticeably shifting from "interview" to "irritated."

His comments surprised me. Contrary to what the administrator seemed to think, I never saw any dancers do drugs, although some weren't shy about sharing that they were on something or other. And as for me personally, I'd never so much as smoked pot. The then president of the

United States had been closer to a joint than I ever had. It wasn't a judgmental thing with me. (After all, you do lose some moral authority when you make most of your income standing around naked in sports socks.) Nor did I think my brain would go all greasy and sunny-side up like in those old "Brain on Drugs" commercials if I dared to try something. It was mostly just that I liked the things I put in my body to come with a brand name, whether it be Coca-Cola or Trojan. I wanted some corporate entity to be responsible in the event something went wrong. (This is also one of the reasons why I shy away from fresh fruits and vegetables.)

Plus, I was always one of those people who could get more than a little loopy from over-the-counter meds. Once I took an especially strong antihistamine and had an experience that seemed strikingly similar to how a friend once described his near-fatal overdose on the horse tranquilizer ketamine. For all these reasons—and not Nancy Reagan—I said no to drugs. So for him to intimate that every stripper was a drug addict was not only wrong, it was personally offensive.

Not only couldn't I believe that he was stereotyping strippers, I also was amazed that someone so ostensibly connected to the gay community could have such a small-minded view of this aspect of the culture. It made me realize that a person's attitude toward stripping and sex work was like a political affiliation. If you were on one side, you found it hard to believe how anyone could have an opposing point of view.

For a few moments, a tense silence hung in the air like the scent of a cheap air freshener: Peevishly Pine.

Finally, he said, "I guess we'll agree to disagree."

"I guess so," I said, just wanting to leave.

He shook my hand, thanked me for coming, and walked me to the door.

When I got home and Seth asked me about the interview, I told him about my confrontation with the administrator. "I'm pretty sure I didn't get the job," I said, "and frankly, after all the bullshit that guy said, I'm not sure if I even want it." I looked at Seth, who was standing over a steaming skillet at the stove. He didn't say anything, but his face was pulled so tight it was like he was trying to give himself a face-lift. Our relationship had become a pressure cooker with no steam valve.

18

A couple of days after my interview, however, things on the home front improved considerably when I got the somewhat surprising news that the job was mine. I could hardly believe this had happened after my tense meeting, but I didn't second-guess my luck. I needed the money and this job made it so that Seth and I would be comfortable even without my stripping income. I called the Follies manager and told him not to put me on the schedule again, but that he'd be seeing me all the time anyway since a big part of my job entailed passing out mini packs of condoms and lube at all the local strip bars, sex clubs, bathhouses, and porn theaters.

I was excited about the job and took it on with an earnest zeal that reminded me of my days as an elementary school patrol. The job proved ideal in many ways because it allowed me to maintain contact with all of my friends and associates at the clubs, even if they did brand me with the unfortunate moniker "Condom Boy."

I wasn't naive enough to think that passing out some free condoms was really going to change anybody's behavior if they were hell-bent on screwing without protection or, as it was becoming known, barebacking, but I was able to use my position to help out some of my friends from the clubs. I had a small budget for developing ads and other educational materials, so I hired a couple of dancers who were photographers and graphic designers to do some work for the program.

I was also able to help in other ways. One day Jay, the dancer I knew from Wet, dropped by the office to see if he could have a roll of condoms. He was on his way to L.A. to make his first porn flick, and the company, which was paying him only about a grand, told him that he had to provide his own penis protectors.

"How cheap can the porn industry be?" I asked Jay.

He laughed, but said that porn was something he'd always wanted to try, and of course, I could relate. But it was another reason why I was glad my porn career never got off the ground.

In addition to being paid to hang out in my old stomping grounds, the job also exposed me to aspects of the local gay sex scene that I wasn't familiar with. Almost every local sex establishment, from bathhouses to members-only parties, welcomed me and my free rubbers. If they ever got in trouble with the cops or community activists, they could use my presence as evidence that they were committed to

AIDS prevention. I was good PR and the job basically gave me the key to the sexual city.

One of my favorite places to visit was a sex party that took place every weekend in a downtown row house. It was fascinating to walk into this normal-looking house and suddenly be thrust into this sexual free-for-all where men were fucking all over the place in all sorts of different ways. In the basement there was a room with lockers where guys would check their clothes—all of their clothes—before proceeding to walk around completely naked with the exception of footwear. Most of the times they'd don sandals, slippers, or flip-flops, all of which made for a nudity-appropriate fashion statement. But occasionally I'd get the odd sight of a naked middle-aged man in nothing but polished black wingtips.

The club's clientele was so fascinating because it wasn't made up of the muscled gym bunnies that dominated so much of the gay scene. Many of these guys had bodies that sagged, jiggled, and poked out in all sorts of undesirable places. Yet they strutted around like Adonises. It was as if they'd transcended conventional ideals of attractiveness or beauty—all things that were obsessions at the strip clubs. They were there simply to fuck on one of the many mattresses that lined the floors of the upstairs bedrooms. Then they'd recover in the living room, where there was a TV and a bar stocked with soda, beer, chips, and liquor.

Being around all this sex gave me a lot of time to reflect on my own sex life—or rather, the relative paucity of it. Although I'd been a stripper and spent many hours being fondled and felt up by strangers, I had still slept with only one guy in my life—Seth. I was increasingly starting to see this as a problem, like maybe I was missing out on something. It wasn't that I wanted to break up. Things had been pretty good since I started having a positive impact on our bank balance again. But I wondered if I would look back and regret not experimenting with other people.

I began broaching the idea that maybe Seth and I could open up our relationship.

"It has nothing to do with my feelings toward you or about the relationship," I explained one night while we were driving home from our favorite Ethiopian restaurant. "But I don't want to someday resent you or even myself for not having had more experiences, you know. You were with other guys before me, but I've never been with anyone else. I think I want that experience. Can you understand that?"

"I mean, I understand," he said, his hand tightly gripped on the steering wheel, his eyes not leaving the road. "But in a way, I don't understand. If you've found the person that you want to be with, why does it matter that you haven't been with other people?"

"I don't know. I just think it does. Or I think that one day it might. I just don't want to have to live with regrets or to feel that I missed out on something."

"Everyone misses out on something. You can't always have it all."

"I'm not trying to have it all," I said, raising my voice a little more than I'd planned. "I'm trying to have something that I want or that I think I might want. And I'm just being upfront and honest about that. I don't want to break up, but I'm asking you to work with me on this."

"Whatever."

"No, you can't just say 'whatever.' How do you feel about this? You have to tell me how you feel."

"I *feel* like you're going to do what you want to do."

"So are you saying it's OK?"

"I don't want to break up, either."

• • • A couple of months passed and we didn't really broach the subject again. I went about doing my job, hanging out and passing out my condoms. It seemed like sexual opportunities were all around me. Stripping had made me more comfortable with my own sexuality, and I longed to see where this newfound confidence could take me. I no longer felt anxious when people came on to me. I felt turned on, alive. I was dying to act upon those feelings, and one Sunday night at the Crew Club, a local bathhouse on the Fourteenth Street corridor where I used to watch the prostitutes strut up and down the block as a kid, I did.

I had been at the club for a couple of hours, had already passed out a number of condoms, and was just hanging out. It was always interesting watching what went on at the club, partly because of the way it was set up. Once you were buzzed in the door and handed a bath towel—it was a bathhouse, after all—you walked through a small mini gym with a bunch of Nautilus machines and some free weights. From there you went into the locker room area. Customers could rent lockers for their clothes or small private rooms—like coat closets with cots—which were located just beyond the public shower. There was also a living room area, where guys could watch TV and flip through magazines, as well as many dark corners and rooms where guys could get it on in semiprivacy. Seeing flocks of men—of all shapes, sizes, ages, and colors—move from area to area, always looking around for the next sexual opportunity, was not unlike watching hamsters—extremely *horny* hamsters—race through a maze.

Whenever I was at the bathhouse, I checked my clothes in a locker and walked around with a towel around my waist so I would blend in. This made the customers more comfortable talking to me about safer sex and the clinic's various services, because I wasn't perceived as an outsider.

On this particular night I spotted a guy I had seen around and always had a crush on. I never acted upon it because of my relationship. But now that I'd had that talk with Seth, things felt very different.

"So, you're passing out condoms tonight?" he asked. His name was Brent and he looked like Archie Andrews from the comics, except way hotter. He had freshly cut reddish brown hair and freckles that playfully dappled the skin that wasn't covered by his towel.

"Yep," I said, turning on the aw-shucks, boy-next-door flirt voice I used with customers. "Care to have one?"

"Sure," he said, slowly taking one from my hand.

"Now, are you sure you know how to use that thing? They can be dangerous in untrained hands."

"Yeah, I think I know what I'm doing. I'm really good at putting them on other people."

"Oh," I said, "so you're more of a receiver than a giver?"

"You could say that," he said, giving me a gleaming smile.

At this point, I was trying to think of anything to keep the conversation going.

"Hey," I continued, "would you say you're a guy who likes to try new things?"

"I guess so. Why?"

"Ever used one of these?" I asked, taking a palm-size plastic packet out of my condom bag.

"What is it?" he asked.

"Well, it's actually a condom that's made for women. You stick it, you know, inside. But a lot of guys are using them now because it's supposed to feel better."

"Why don't you show me how it works? I have a room down the hall."

"Um, sure," I said.

I followed him through the hallways filled with shirtless, towel-clad men, their eyes springing to life every time a new face passed by. We made it to his room, closed the door, dimmed the lights. We both dropped our towels, and my dick sprang to attention like something that should've come with a cartoonish *boiiiiing* sound.

"There's a special technique to putting it in," I said. "Why don't you bend over for me."

He leaned his body over the small cot in the room, spread

his freckled ass cheeks, and looked back over his shoulder, smiling. I popped open one of my mini tubes of lube and started greasing up his ass. He wiggled his butt as my fingers moved around and I could see goose pimples pop up on his skin. I took the female condom—a sandwich bag–looking thing with a plastic ring in it—and slowly worked it in with my fingers. He moaned and started playing with his cock. I moved my fingers in and out, in and out, faster and faster, and used my other hand to jerk my cock. We stayed like this for what could've been ten minutes or just about ninety seconds. It all happened in sex time, where things speed up, slow to a crawl, and sometimes suspend entirely in ways that have nothing to do with what's going on with the clock.

When it was over and we were spent, we wiped ourselves off with our towels and exchanged some completely innocuous but good-natured small talk. It felt less like we had just had sex than like we were running buddies and had just completed one of our weekly runs. We got dressed, dropped our used towels in the big dirty towel bin by the door, and walked out to the street together. I thought about giving him a hug before we parted but decided against it. As we headed to our respective cars, we both agreed that "it was fun."

I got home and told Seth all about it, every moment, every detail. I felt that I could win some goodwill points by at least being completely honest. My best hope was that he wouldn't think finger fucking some guy with a female condom was all that big of a deal, but I left myself open for the possibility that he might be really pissed at me for a while. What I didn't expect was that he'd start crying and keep crying for hours. No matter how I tried to assure him that what happened had nothing to do with my feelings for him, he wouldn't stop sobbing. As I reluctantly fell into sleep, the sound of him crying was still in my ears. The next morning, he canceled his classes at school and spent the day in bed. That evening, he asked me to move out.

His request shocked me. I couldn't believe that what was so insignificant in my mind had led him to such a life-changing decision. Why couldn't he be cool with this like he had been with everything else? Where was my second chance?

We spent the next few days not really speaking except when absolutely necessary, as I went about looking for a new place to live and he took extraordinary efforts to be home as little as possible, staying late at the school library and catching up with friends he hadn't seen in years. But even though we didn't talk, we still managed to communicate, most effectively through Mariah Carey's latest CD, *Butterfly*. I repeatedly played the title track and would loudly sing along to the lyrics: "Wild horses run unbridled / Or their spirit dies." Seth would then walk to the CD player and calmly advance the disc four tracks to "Breakdown."

As the song played, I'd hear him singing from another room, "So what do you do when / somebody you're so devoted to / Suddenly just stops loving you / And it seems they haven't got a clue." This back-and-forth duel with Mariah spoke loads about our relationship. We were similar in so many ways, yet far apart in others, the same artist singing two different songs.

"So this is what you really want?" I asked him early the next Saturday morning, a U-Haul packed with my boxes waiting in the parking lot outside.

"Can you say that you're never going to have sex with another guy again?" he asked, looking up, his red eyes meeting mine.

"I want to be able to say that. I really do. But I'm not sure that I can. It wouldn't be the truth. And I don't want to lie to you. I've never lied to you."

Seth paused, looked away, and said, "I think this is the best thing."

We were at an impasse—the first in seven years that we weren't able to get around together.

I moved into an apartment in downtown D.C. and started experiencing a number of things I'd been so curious about trying: picking up a hot guy at a club, bringing him home, programming some of Madonna's slower stuff on the multidisc CD player ("Shoo-Bee-Doo" from *Like a Virgin*, "Inside of Me" and "Forbidden Love" from *Bedtime Stories*), and hungrily learning the secrets of a new body.

But, at the same time, I missed Seth and a lot of things about being in a relationship, like the sense that I belonged to someone and that we were building a life together. I didn't know how to reconcile this with my growing need for independence, with the feeling that this might be my last chance to find out who I am on my own terms.

I also quickly learned something else I hadn't quite expected: how friggin' expensive it was to live alone. My rent was more than what Seth and I had been paying combined, and all the other bills that I was used to splitting—phone, cable, and the rest—I now had to handle on my own. My entire paycheck would be spent by the time I got it, so despite the new job, where I was supposed to be a role model and representative of one of the most prestigious AIDS organizations in the country, I had to secretly return to the one thing I knew could bring me fast money: stripping.

19

O nce I started dancing again, there was a Redd Foxx joke that often ran through my mind. A sofa salesman says to a woman at a bar, "If the furniture business don't get no better, I'm gonna lose my ass." The woman turns to the man and says, "Well, if the ass business don't get no better, I'm gonna lose my furniture."

This perfectly summed up my situation. I was no longer baring my ass as a way to experience something different or to discover something about myself and my sexuality. This was all about rent, the electric bill, the phone bill, the cable bill, the gym membership (a luxury for some, but an urban gay male essential), groceries, restaurant takeout, books, CDs, and clothes—in other words, the life to which I'd become accustomed, only now I had to make it work all on my own.

I decided to start back at the Follies, even though I knew that dancers at the other clubs were making good money again now that customers had resigned themselves to the permanence of "The Rule." But I once again needed the anonymity of the Follies, which was still a "You don't tell and I won't tell" kind of place. I couldn't risk being discovered because I was certain I'd lose my job if anyone at the clinic found out I was stripping. I knew that the clinic was too big a public organization to risk the bad PR of having its head of gay outreach booty-shaking for tips at the local porn house.

The surprising and unexpected thing about becoming a stripper again, however, was that in many ways it made me more effective at reaching others about the clinic's services. Before, when I walked through the club with my bag of rubbers, I was dismissed—albeit playfully—as Condom Boy. But now that I was stripping again, I had other strippers and even customers come up to me all the time asking for condoms or info about HIV and STD testing. One time, another dancer pulled me into a corner and whipped out his dick, which had a dime-sized purple blister to the left of his pee hole. "Do you think this is something I should get looked at?" he asked as I tried to pop my eyes back into my head.

I told Seth—whom I still spoke to about once a week—that stripping was making me better at my job, but he responded, irritated, "Craig, you would still be stripping even if it wasn't." I wouldn't have admitted it to him, but he was right. He generally was when it came to stuff that was going on with me, and that's why I still needed him in my life. I was determined for us to find some way to maintain a friendship. So I called him regularly to tell him how broke I was and generally how sucky my life had become. I figured that on some level, he must enjoy hearing about my hard times, and it was the least I could do to keep him updated.

The truth was that things had taken a turn for the shitty. In my new apartment, I hung up a photo that I cut out of the *Washington Post* of R&B singer Mary J. Blige consoling her friend rapper Lil' Kim at the funeral of Kim's ex-boyfriend the Notorious B.I.G. The things I was going through were in no way equivalent to their experience, but I could still relate to the sense of loss, the awareness that something was gone and things would never be the same.

I wasn't even enjoying having sex anymore, yet I was hooking up constantly. For the first time, I even got together with other dancers. One Sunday I was working with a choirboy-faced dancer named Glen, who'd just gotten out of prison for drunk driving and pot possession. We went back to my apartment and fucked between every set. It was fun, but it wasn't half as enjoyable as that woozy feeling I used to get around Mikey and other dancers that I had nursed crushes on. The problem was that it was harder to crush on people when you were actually available to act on those feelings. There was no more mystery. Sex had taken on a harder edge.

One night I picked up a flight attendant at Secrets and we raced back to his hotel and got wasted on mini bottles of vodka that he'd lifted from his last flight. (I'd also started drinking since the breakup. It was another new thing I was trying.) I pounded his ass so hard that my crotch was sore for days. I felt the way I did when I strained a muscle at the gym. Sex had become sport. It was all stamina and endurance and pushing beyond my limits. But I missed the days when it used to be fun.

I wasn't taking much pleasure in anything, especially stripping. Where working for twelve hours at the Follies used to feel like a day at a kinky day camp, it now was torturous—not quite a bamboo shoot in the penis, but irritating, like water constantly dripping on my head. And none of my old hanging buddies like Danny or Mikey were around anymore. Like so many other dancers, they just disappeared from the scene.

One Sunday night around 11 PM, I was sitting in the Follies lobby killing time before the midnight show. I couldn't wait to finish up, go home, shower, and try to get some sleep before I had to get up in time to make it to the clinic by 9 AM.

My eyes were staring at the TV, which was showing the local evening news. Red-and-blue lights were flashing on a darkened street. Yellow crime scene tape stretched between streetlamps. I couldn't hear what was going on, but the message was clear: somebody somewhere wouldn't be seeing tomorrow.

As I watched the screen, I heard the click of the circular entrance bar. In walked Dave, who I hadn't seen in a couple of months. This was odd since I used to run into him just about every weekend.

I gave him a nod and he came over and sat next to me. We didn't shake hands, hug, or do any of the other things that friends or even close acquaintances do when greeting each other. We never did these things. I hadn't thought about it before, but suddenly this struck me as odd. Over the years, Dave had probably spent hours with my dick in his hand, and I knew all sorts of details about his sex life, past and present. Yet we never touched, even casually, unless I was dancing and he was tipping. Those were the unspoken rules, and we were veterans at the game.

"Hey, stranger," I said. "Where have you been?"

He laughed. "Well, for one, Peter hasn't been around," he said.

"Yeah, I haven't seen him in a while, but you know how it is. Guys come and go. Then they come back again. Then go again. And so on and so on."

"What about you? You're back dancing?"

"Yep. I needed the cash."

"Are you still at the clinic?"

"Yeah, but ssshhh," I said, putting my finger over my mouth. "I've been dancing again for a few weeks now and thought it was weird that I hadn't seen you."

"Well, for a while, I was seeing somebody."

"Really? A dancer?"

"No, just a regular guy. It wasn't that serious. Just sort of hanging out. We'd try to get together on weekends, but if for some reason we didn't, it was no big deal. We kept it real casual. But then one day out of the blue, he asked if I'd be interested in a one-on-one, monogamous-type relationship."

"What did you say?" I asked.

"I had to tell him that it wasn't going to work for me. I mean, he's a wonderful person, very nice. Let's say I was sick and got AIDS or something and needed somebody to take care of me; I think that he would do that. He's that kind of guy."

"So, what's the problem?"

Dave paused a moment and leaned back on the couch. "Well, he's forty, and that's way out of my normal range. It's just the way it is for me. I mean, a guy can be responsible, have a good job, and be a very kind person. But if he's over, say, twenty-five, it ain't gonna fly. I might like him as a friend. But I won't want to keep having sex with him because I won't be able to keep getting a hard-on. It's that simple."

"You broke up with him?"

"We didn't have that kind of relationship. We just stopped doing it."

"And now you're back to your familiar turf," I said, trying to lighten things a little.

"No, that was a couple of months ago, but I still haven't been out that much. The last few times I was out, I didn't really have a good time. I don't know. I left thinking, 'This is superficial. This is extremely superficial. These guys don't give a shit about you. They just want your money.'"

Hearing this from Dave surprised me. He always said that the clubs gave him almost everything he was looking for in terms of sex and companionship. But something had changed.

"Look at our relationship," he continued. "I think you

like me and I certainly like you. And whenever we see each other, we always have a nice conversation; and if I haven't seen you in a while, I think, 'I haven't seen Craig around lately.' But that's where it stops. I don't know anything else about you. I don't even know your last name. I couldn't have called you if I needed some help or just wanted to get in touch or whatever. It all stops here, and that's what I mean by superficiality."

I didn't know what to say. I felt a little attacked. It was like Dave was breaking a contract or something. I did genuinely like him and enjoyed talking to him. But what we had at the clubs was enough for me. Was that wrong?

I turned my head back to the TV as if the "Sports Blooper of the Week" demanded my full attention.

"But when I start feeling like this I try not to dwell on it," he said. "I used to have this theory that many more dramatic bad things were going to happen to you in life than dramatic good things. But a friend once told me that the key was to look for the good in small things, like a sunrise or something like that. And I try practicing that. But sometimes it gets hard."

We chatted a little more after that. I updated him on the new dancers that I thought he'd like and told him that "The Rule" was still in effect at the other clubs. Then I left the lobby to get ready for the midnight show. On the way back to the dressing room, the D.J. asked me what I wanted him to play for my set. "Whatever," I said. As Tina Turner once sang, "I'm your private dancer . . . and any old music will do."

When I walked out onto the stage that night, I didn't even bother with my normal thirty seconds of two-stepping from side to side. I dropped my jean shorts and stepped right out into the audience. There were only three people in the theater. One was a fat, hairy-chested white guy who was leaning against the wall playing with his cock. Another was a disturbingly thin man who, when I walked past him earlier, smelled like formaldehyde. And then there was Dave seated in the center.

I avoided the other customers and went right over to Dave. He smiled. I lifted my left leg and he placed a wad of folded bills into my sock. Usually, at this point, I stayed standing as he worked me over with his hands, but this time, I opened my legs, put my full weight on his lap, and pressed close to him, placing my arms on his shoulders. He grabbed my dick firmly and moved his hand steadily up and down as I continued to push my weight into him. We stayed like that for my whole set until the last song faded. And as I got up, I put my arms around him and gave him a hug. He smiled again and slapped my ass as I walked away.

It wasn't long after that night that I decided—once again—I had to quit, not just dancing, but the whole life I was trying to lead. It wasn't working. I couldn't afford to just work at the clinic, and I didn't want to dance anymore. I didn't want to grow to hate it. Besides, I was about to turn thirty and stripping is a *Logan's Run*-ish sort of job. I didn't want to step onstage one day and suddenly burst into flames or, nearly as bad, become one of those older dancers who were often the butt of customers' jokes.

There was one thirty-something dancer who looked a fresh-faced twenty-four except when he smiled and you could see the deeply etched crow's feet around his eyes. I once heard a customer quip that it looked like a cat had attacked him. I didn't want people talking about me like that.

But even more, I felt it was time to reboot my entire life and really try to pursue my dream of writing. My mom, who now lived out of state, told me that I could move in with her until I decided what I wanted to do, so I started making plans to temporarily leave town.

I gave notice at the clinic and signed up for my last time dancing at the Follies. The theater's twenty-fifth anniversary was coming up and I decided to make my last appearance at the accompanying celebration. It made perfect full-circle sense. I'd started at the Follies and it was where my stripping adventure would end.

On the night of the anniversary party, the Follies was more crowded than I'd ever seen it. Dozens of guys filled the lobby and the theater. The attendees reflected a mix of regulars and local gay VIPs who'd all been specially selected for this invitation-only evening-wear event. Although the Follies existed on the redheaded stepchild periphery of the gay community most of the time, it took on a certain nostalgic charm during its annual anniversary celebration. The theater had been a D.C. gay fixture for more than two decades, through the fire that killed nine, the death of the original owner—and later his namesake son, who was gay and died of AIDS—and then all the raids and scrutiny that dramatically changed the vibe of the other strip joints. The Follies had survived it all.

That night, as the crowd of older men, dressed almost uniformly in suits, ties, and shiny shoes, milled around, eating from the buffet and drinking from the open bar, they talked about how this wasn't really the theater's twenty-fifth anniversary at all. The Follies opened in the fall of 1974, which would have only made it twenty-four. But several years back someone made a clerical mistake, bumping the theater's age up a year. Everyone knew about the error, but no one wanted to repeat an anniversary party or, even worse, skip one. And to some extent, it didn't matter anyway. The Follies' main appeal had always been about fantasy and the suspension of disbelief.

About an hour after the party started, the show began and the guests moved from the lobby into the theater, which was decidedly less dirty and crotchy than usual. "Gentlemen," the announcer said over the loudspeaker, "welcome to the twenty-fourth, well, twenty-fifth anniversary of the Follies." Then the music started—I don't remember the song—and I walked onstage with about ten other dancers who'd been handpicked for the party. We were all dressed in black G-strings and bow ties, the stripper equivalent of formal wear. Because this was a mixed crowd of regulars and local luminaries, we didn't have to take anything off. We just walked through the crowd collecting tips. Things felt so different from when I first stepped onto this stage a few years earlier. Then it seemed like I was entering a strange, smelly, scary new world; now, I was leaving home.

I deliberately didn't say that this was my last night to any of the customers, even Dave, who I spotted smiling as he talked in the corner with Peter, who had returned just to dance at the party.

The show lasted only ten minutes. It was over before I could even tell myself to really feel what was going on, to really remember the experience because it was going to be my last time. I went back to the dressing room, put on my dress shirt and black pants, and my entire memory of the show vanished like a puff of breath on a winter's day.

I made my exit quickly, saying good-bye only to those people who happened to be in my path to the door. But as I left the theater and took that familiar walk down the dark, litter-strewn street to my car, I heard a voice call out from behind me. It was the Follies' manager. He'd forgotten to give me the framed photo that they used to advertise my appearance at the party. He handed me the cheap, plastic pop-in frame with the picture of me smiling widely, and "Craig" written in showy cursive above my head. I looked so happy. I thanked him and said good-bye again.

I continued toward my car, and as I walked farther and farther away from the theater, this strange feeling rose inside me. I was sad, but in a hard-to-pin-down way. Sure, I'd felt ready to quit stripping for a while now, but the finality of it felt so, well, final. There was a voice in my head saying over and over again, with a James Earl Jones–ish thunder, "No matter what else you will become in life, you will never be this again."

20

I was sitting in a small room on the outskirts of Minneapolis talking to pop superstar Janet Jackson
about masturbation. It reminded me of one of those
moments when I'd be stripping and think, "How did my
life lead me here?" Of course, I'd made strategic decisions
to get to these places. But I still felt awestruck that I'd actually done it, that I was living a dream. Oprah has her "Aha"
moments; these were my "Holy fuck" moments.

The reason I was talking to Janet—and she was letting
me get all up in her business without cursing me out or
kicking me in the nuts—was for a *VIBE* magazine cover
story. It marked my biggest accomplishment yet in a career
that I first started thinking about while at the clubs, flipping through *Entertainment Weekly* and other magazines
between sets.

Shortly after I stopped dancing at the Follies, I began
writing a music column for a D.C. gay club 'zine, *Metro*

Weekly. I did it for free, but I liked the exposure and it was good practice. Not long after that, I placed my first review in the *Village Voice,* which has served as the training den for almost all the major pop music critics. I got this gig by writing the music editor a letter explaining that I was an aspiring music critic/stripper. I sent this along with some of my *Metro Weekly* reviews. The editor called me about a week later and said that while he hated my reviews, he was intrigued by my letter. He decided to give me a shot and a couple of weeks later my first review appeared in the *Voice.*

The fact that I got this gig in part because I'd told the editor that I used to be a stripper was life-changing for me in ways that I couldn't fully appreciate at the time. When I started stripping, I thought that I'd have doors closed to me because of what I was doing, but I did it anyway because I felt it was something I needed to do. Now, stripping was actually opening a door for me, potentially leading me to a whole new world of opportunity. I became a firm believer in the power of taking risks.

After being published in the *Village Voice,* I started reaching out to other publications and was soon writing for the *Washington Post, Spin,* and *VIBE.* I'd also moved from simply penning reviews to writing feature articles where I had to interview various music artists. I found my stripping experience came in handy when talking to celebs. After years of working the bars and making small talk while people were playing with my dick, I'd learned something about relating to people—how to lean forward when they were speaking and look deeply into their eyes, and how to listen closely to what they were saying in order to get a sense of where they were coming from.

I relied on these skills very early on as I found myself talking with celebrities whom I was by no means qualified or experienced enough to be interviewing. One of my first big feature assignments was to interview Mariah Carey for the *Washington Post* in 1999. Mariah had recently divorced her Svengali hubby, Sony Music's head honcho, Tommy Mottola, and was about to release a new album, *Rainbow*. It was the follow-up to 1997's *Butterfly*, an album which featured contributions from rappers Sean "Puffy" Combs, Bone Thugs-N-Harmony, and Missy Elliott, and brought her criticism from people thinking she was a pop princess trying to go hip-hop.

The plan was for me to take the train up to New York and then spend much of the evening watching Mariah flounce around doing her trademark diva thing. But I almost messed things up from the start. I arrived at a nondescript row house on a cobblestone street in lower Manhattan. It was some kind of boutique editing facility, where Mariah was overseeing one of her new videos. The guy who answered the doorbell told me to wait downstairs and that Mariah would be with me "shortly." So I sat on the leather couch and flipped through my notebook of questions and checked to make sure my tape recorder worked. "Shortly" became fifteen minutes, then thirty, then forty-five.

Finally, the guy who'd answered the door came back in the room.

"Mariah wants to meet you," he said.

"OK," I said. "Should I bring all my stuff with me, or can I leave it here?"

"Leave it here," he said, referring to my backpack, which had my notes and tape recorder in it.

I followed the guy up the stairs. With each step, I thought, I'm getting closer and closer to meeting Mariah. I was, after all, a huge fan, having stripped several times to "Fantasy" and hearing my breakup with Seth played out in songs like "Butterfly" and "Breakdown."

We reached the top of the staircase and entered a room where Mariah, dressed in an olive midriff-baring top and jeans, sat in front of a small video monitor along with three or four other people. As I walked in the door, she looked up at me with an expression not unlike that of a dog wondering who's going to be next to kick it.

The guy who brought me in gestured for me to sit on a worn black leather couch in the back of the room. He walked over to Mariah, took her hand, and led her over to where I was sitting. Like most celebrities, she looked smaller in person—thinner, I could report to my cattier friends.

"This is Mariah," he said, as if there was some question about this, like instead he was going to introduce me to her secret twin sister, Moira.

"How's it goin'?" I asked.

"Fine," she answered breathily, shaking my hand and sitting on the couch next to me. "Let me just preface this whole thing by saying how tired I am. Did they brief you on what my day's been like?"

"Uh, no," I said.

"I've done two major interviews. And I went to bed at seven-thirty AM because I was editing another video with Sanaa [Hamri], my friend, my Moroccan homegirl, my biracial homegirl. And all the while, I've been approving photos and doing phoners for the Italian press. So I'm kinda exhausted. And I'm just saying that because if I come across a little strange, that's why. A lot of reporters try to take advantage of that and try to make me sound crazy."

"I understand," I said.

Mariah then started talking. And talking. And talking. She launched into a ten-minute, nonstop stream-of-consciousness soliloquy that rushed from why she needed to finish this video before she headed to Japan to all the work she's been doing to finish her album to all the stress that she's been under trying to keep her career going in the wake of her divorce to all of the selfless things that she does that people don't know about like taking care of a nephew who she's putting through college and who she's so proud of because he's on the honor roll and . . .

Suddenly she stopped. "Are you going to write any of this down?" she asked me.

"Oh," I said. "I didn't realize we were going to do the interview now. I left all my stuff downstairs."

"Well, why did you let me go on and on, wasting my voice like this?" she asked. "I shouldn't be wasting my voice like this. Speaking tires out my voice and I should be resting my voice."

"Sorry," I said. "I'll go get my stuff."

I got up, raced down the steps, grabbed my bag, and headed back to the room. When I returned, Mariah was in front of the monitors again. She didn't look at me as I walked over to the couch and waited in silence.

About thirty minutes later, her personal assistant, a meek, white-haired woman, came over and told me that Mariah needed to go to a studio in midtown and that she would talk to me on the ride over.

"Cool," I said.

Not long afterward, I followed her small entourage outside to the street, where a black stretch limo and two black SUVs waited.

"You'll ride with Mariah in the limo," the assistant instructed.

I waited as the driver opened the door for the singer and then I followed her in.

"People always criticize me for riding in a limo," she said as I sat across from her, "but it's just that I have so much stuff to carry around and it's easiest to just throw it in the limo."

I made no mention of the fact that the only things in the limo were me, her, and my bag. At this point, I was just trying to regain my ground so that she'd believe I was an established journalist and not some guy who'd gotten to interview her as a fluke of fate, which actually was closer to the truth. I took out my tape recorder and notebook. I was about to speak when, out of nowhere, she blurted out, "Can I ask you a question just because I'm, like, obsessed with this? What nationality are you?"

"What?" I thought. I was familiar with Mariah's story—the daughter of an Irish mother and a father who was part black/part Venezuelan; when her parents married, Mariah's mother was disowned by her family; drama ensued. But my mind went back to all the times in the clubs when a customer would ask my race, and depending on my response would decide whether or not to keep tipping me. It was admittedly a sore spot, and I answered, "I'm black," with perhaps more attitude than I intended.

"Oh, I was just asking because you look like you might be biracial."

"Well, I'm not," I said. "I'm black. Both of my parents are black."

I looked at her and could tell that I had made yet another mistake. It was as if we were two kids on the elementary school playground. She had asked to be my friend and I had pushed her face-first into the sandbox.

Fuck! I was new at this so I didn't know the best way to develop rapport with a celebrity, but I was sure this wasn't it. I was screwing up. What should I do? I glanced over at my questions.

"Are you still going in a hip-hop direction with this album?" I asked.

"People just bring me down when they ask questions like that," she answered. "As a songwriter, I'm capable of writing more mainstream stuff or making a hip-hop record or a house record or probably a country song. Or even, like, no one knows this, but I've written some alternative things. I'm just pretty much 'whatever.'"

I looked back at my questions and they all seemed to suck: "What are you trying to accomplish with the new album?" "Which producers did you work with?" I couldn't ask her these questions. They just didn't go with the mood. I wasn't dealing with somebody who was in cool professional mode. This was a woman who was all over the place, jumping from mood to mood, thought to thought.

I wondered how I would've dealt with it if she had been a guy coming up to me at the bar. How would I have made a connection? I put my questions away.

"So, it seems like you're kind of having a long day," I said.

She sighed deeply, her whole body heaving up and down.

"I'm sorry," she said, explaining the sigh. "I'm relaxing. This is my way of relaxing."

I didn't say anything.

"I'm just explaining to you where I was then," she said. "That's one zone. But now I'm going into the Craig zone."

"OK," I said, thinking this is getting weirder by the second. "So, it's been a long day?"

She sighed again.

"I am so hungry," she said.

"Why don't you get something to eat?"

"Oh, they're getting me something," she said, referring to, I assumed, the group of about five people who were constantly scurrying around her at the editing studio. "But

I'm just sick of it. I eat at the same places almost every night."

"Why are you working so hard?" I asked. After all, she had sold millions of albums and had more number one pop singles than any woman in history.

She was quiet for a few moments. Then she said, "It's just something I feel like I have to do. It's something I've always felt like I had to do. I have an overblown insecure streak that runs through me, and sometimes it manifests itself as me being a workaholic. I just work, and I think it's because in the early part of my life, I felt like I had to always scramble. I didn't have any stability. And I didn't know what was going on in my life. So I feel like I have to keep going, probably because I'm insecure and I feel like I have to maintain how far I've come."

"So, it really has to do with how you grew up?"

"My reality is that I grew up as an interracial child. My reality is that I grew up with a lot of disturbing imagery around me, a lot of stuff that most kids in suburbia did not see. I grew up very fast in terms of my perception of the world and my understanding of what it's like to be mixed and to hear how white people speak about black people when they're not in the room and vice versa."

"And this affected how you thought about yourself?"

"I felt like, if my mother's family disowned my mom because of this, what does that make me?"

This became the theme of our whole talk. I wasn't getting Mariah the ultrademanding diva, but an insecure person with something to prove. I could relate.

When I turned in my article to the *Post*, I presented a picture of a pop diva who was out of touch with her own success, who was working herself nutty because she still felt that after all she'd accomplished, it could be taken away at any moment. The *Post* editor hated it. She had a hard time believing that this pampered pop star was really dealing with demons. "No, really, you wouldn't believe how messed-up she seems," I argued. The editor remained unconvinced, but the piece ran anyway. One year later, Mariah was hospitalized for exhaustion.

This Mariah story led to other assignments and I started trusting my instincts more. One day I got the call from *Spin* magazine asking me to write a piece on Mary J. Blige, the hip-hop soul Cinderella who rose from the Yonkers projects to the top of the charts. The *Spin* editors had chosen Blige's 1994 effort, *My Life*—a searing confessional chronicling her tumultuous relationship with K-Ci Hailey, front man for the bad-boy R&B quartet Jodeci—as one of its "Top 100 Albums of the 90s." I was all for it because I had loved Blige's music since her 1992 debut, *What's the 411?*

Right after that album came out, I saw Blige in concert and, at the show, I bought a baseball hat that had her signature running across the top. I wore the hat everywhere, and one day, as I walked into the Martin Luther King Jr. Library to do research, a young black woman stopped me, looked at my hat, twisted up her face, and said, "Dag, you like her *that* much?" Well, yes, I did, and my feelings hadn't changed.

Nevertheless, I was a little worried about the interview. Mary had a reputation for being a difficult subject. Sometimes she would shut down completely; other times she could be downright combative, once even challenging supermodel/journalist Veronica Webb to a fistfight. I figured that I'd be physically safe since our interview was taking place by phone. As far as I knew, you couldn't wirelessly transmit a bitch slap. But still, I worried about getting the information I needed.

The interview started awkwardly. My job was to get Mary to talk about the making of the album, so after introducing myself and exchanging "How you doin's," I asked, "So, do you need any special things in the studio when you record, like candles or anything?"

"No, I don't need some strange atmosphere with incense and candles and all of that shit," she snapped. "It's not about a candle and making an atmosphere because the atmosphere is in me."

OK, I thought, not sure what to make of Mary's inner atmosphere. Although I couldn't see her face, I felt from her tone that something was on her mind—something bigger and deeper than any album. And rather than take her prickliness personally, I decided to change direction and just ask about what was going on in her life. Maybe then she'd warm up and feel comfortable discussing the album.

"Do you ever feel like you're misunderstood? It seems like people always have negative stuff to say about you."

"Yes," she said. I could hear her take a breath. "People look at my past and say, 'Well, she's from a grimy element so she's gotta be grimy, too.' But you never judge a book by its cover or people by the company they're around, you know, because Jesus was around bad company but he was one of the lambs."

"Were you dealing with people thinking bad things about you when you were making *My Life*?"

"*My Life* was one of the most hard times of my career. That album was written out of tears. I was just going through it and wondering why I'm not being treated the right way. Most of the times I wrote, I was at home. And I would just sit there writing my feelings down because the paper was all I had to talk to."

"You were writing down things you felt you couldn't say?"

"Like in the song 'Be With You,' in so many words, I was talking to my little cousin. I was telling him that I don't understand why every time I come around, everybody's angry, nobody wants me around, and everybody treats me so bad and everybody's so jealous and mad because God's blessing me."

"And were you also writing about problems in a romantic relationship? Was that inspired by real life, too?"

"It's all real, man. There's no bullshit on the album. Because I was really hurt. I'm not an opportunist. I don't take the bad times and use that as an opportunity to look like a hero. I was really suffering. *My Life* is straight heartache and pain. Listening to the album, you definitely hear that Mary was a troubled young woman. I just didn't know a lot of the things I know now. It was a hurtful time for me because I was trying to find me. All of my troubles and all of my fears were because of me. But all the abuse and all the rest of that stuff was so unnecessary. Why would you just do somebody like me like that? Because I don't hurt people unless they hurt me.

"But," she continued, "I think that first relationship taught me to see what kind of people are after me—users, opportunists, men that just want to use you and abuse you and shoot you down in your career. They gotta make you feel lesser than them so that they can feel strong."

"So, you feel like you learned some lessons from the experiences you sang about on *My Life*?" I asked, a bit shocked that she was being so forthcoming.

"No, I made a mistake and here I am again. You can be with somebody and you think they love you, but all along they're really jealous and mad and they really hate you. So, I've been used up again because somebody just didn't care enough to treat me like somebody and understand my struggle, saying, 'Let me give this girl the happiness she deserves and make her feel really good and treat her like somebody, let me trust her, let me love her, let me not third-degree her, let me give her what she wants.' I got none of that. All I got was bullshit, being cheated on, being lied to, shut down, being told that I wasn't shit but a ho, being looked at as a ho, always women being compared to me."

She paused for a few seconds. I wasn't sure whether to ask another question or wait.

"It sounds like you're going through the same struggle again—"

"I know we're doing an interview right now," she said.

"But I'm really fucking hurt right now, really messed up *today*. It's the same shit, just a different nigga with a different way of bringing it."

We talked for several more minutes, as Mary chronicled in detail many of the issues that she was having with her current boyfriend. As the conversation continued, I was struck by how hurt she was by these guys who had taken her for granted and cheated on her. Then, all of a sudden, a thought hit me. "Oh, fuck, am I one of those guys? Am I that type of asshole?"

As soon as the interview was over, and I thanked Mary for her openness and wished her the best, I popped open my cell phone again and phoned Seth. He had recently moved into a new apartment, a place that was decidedly more bachelor-homo chic than my dorm-room–like abode.

"Everything is cool between us, right?" I asked as soon as he answered.

"What? What do you mean?"

"I mean, like, everything. Like us. We're cool, right?"

"What is this all about?"

"Nothing. I mean, you know how much I care about you, right?"

"I know," he said, giving me his usual indulgent sigh.

"And you know that I never meant to hurt you and would never intentionally try to hurt you, like, ever?"

"I know."

"I just wanted to make sure . . ."

"We're fine. But I have someone over for dinner. Let me call you later. OK?"

"Is it a date?"

"Let me call you later."

"OK," I said, snapping the cover closed on my cell phone.

I sat in silence for a few minutes. I was really jealous about Seth's date. But at the same time, I was happy for him. That was the way things often felt in my relationship with Seth—good, but all mixed up. I figured this was just the way it was to have a complicated history with somebody. And I imagined that this was the way things would always be.

By the time the *Spin* article came out, I was starting to get noticed as a writer, and pretty soon I landed my dream job working at *Entertainment Weekly*. I was hired as a correspondent for the website, but I also got to write pieces for the magazine. Taking this job meant leaving D.C. for New York, a move that felt weird because, save for my brief stint living in New York before college, I'd never really thought about permanently moving from D.C. again. I just figured I would always live there. After all, the city had allowed me to be so many different things: juvenile TV personality, grad student, stripper, AIDS educator. But in order to play in the entertainment journalism major leagues, I had to leave home.

Other things were different as well. By this point, I wasn't as open about my time stripping as I had been when I approached the *Village Voice*. The more success I achieved as a writer, the more I felt like I had to play the role of a serious young journalist, not the type of guy who would romp around a nightclub with his dick out. Perhaps as a defensive overcompensation for my nude dancing days, I showed up for my first day at *Entertainment Weekly* decked out in the only suit I owned, a Kuppenheimer original, paired with a tie I'd borrowed from Seth. This made a distinctive first impression, though not exactly the kind I was going for, since everyone else was walking around in jeans and khakis.

Being a full-time journalist was a lot different from working as a freelancer. There were so many writers and it was quite a competitive environment. Yet I quickly—and somewhat unexpectedly—found my niche because of the ease I had asking celebrities extremely personal questions, especially those having to do with sex and relationships. The funny thing was that I didn't perceive this as anything special. After years of working at strip clubs I had lost a sense of polite conversation. Nothing felt out of bounds to say or ask. It was just sex. Everybody's doing it or wants to do it. What's the big deal?

I discovered my aptitude for this type of questioning one day while I was doing a phone interview with a teenage Bonnie Raitt in training named Shannon Curfman. She was being billed as the anti-Britney because she wrote her own songs and was handy with a guitar. But beyond all of that, I mostly agreed to the interview because my editor had a jailbait crush on her. Besides, she was rumored to be dating two striking blonds—Jonny Lang, another blues-rock prodigy, and one of the Hanson brothers. I wanted to get to the bottom of it.

She called me from a steak house where she was eating while on tour, and after a couple of softball questions about her album, I jumped in to see what was really going on in her teenage love life.

"So, what's the deal with you and Jonny Lang?"

"Nothing. He cowrote a song on my album. But he's more like a brother."

"Oh, well, speaking of brothers, what about those Hanson boys?"

"What about them?"

"Would you describe your relationship with any of them as not 'like a brother'?"

"I'm not saying anything."

"That sounds pretty suspicious."

She laughed. "Yeah, well."

"Well, the rumor is you're dating Zac."

"Zac, really? I've never heard that."

"OK. So, then it's Isaac."

"No."

"Then it must be Taylor."

She laughed again. "I told you I'm not saying."

We went on and on like this for about five minutes, after I had pretty much narrowed her brotherly blond du jour to Taylor. After I hung up, I realized that my editor had been listening to the interview from the next cubicle. This made me nervous. Did I go too far prying into this tenth-grader's love life? He came over and had a rather stern look on his face. I thought he was mad about something.

"I'm the most persistent reporter I know, but you asked

those Hanson questions about ten times more than I would've," he said. At first, I wasn't sure how to take what he said, but then he cracked a smile and I figured I'd done good.

I think what made me good at asking personal questions was not only that I was used to talking to people about the most intimate aspects of their lives and had no qualms asking about anything that piqued my curiosity, but also that I was used to making people comfortable in uncomfortable or awkward situations. When someone is playing with your dick in public, it's not only potentially awkward for you, the one being played with, it can also be weird for the person doing the playing, because he is exposing his desires so nakedly in front of other people. He loses a certain anonymity that comes with being at a nightclub. The customer goes from being a face in a crowd to being a hand on your dick. It has the effect of having your secret crush revealed in the high school auditorium. In fact, it wasn't at all surprising, after a customer felt you up, for him to rush off to the bathroom, another part of the club, or even head home.

I think customers sometimes felt more exposed than I did. Part of being a good stripper involved putting the customers at ease with what they were doing—otherwise their discomfort could lessen how much they tipped. At the clubs, I tried to laugh a lot and bring some sort of humor to every situation with a customer, and this same approach got me out of a lot of tight spots when interviewing celebrities.

In fact, the only time at *Entertainment Weekly* that I remember a celebrity getting upset with me for asking too many personal questions was when I was interviewing German supermodel Heidi Klum before a Victoria's Secret show.

"What kind of underwear do you like on a guy? Boxers or briefs?" I asked.

"I like briefs. They're sexier. They form the body. I think with boxers, you're hiding something because everything is so loose."

"Does your husband wear briefs?"

"Let's not talk about my husband's briefs too much," she snapped in her clipped Germlish.

I spent about a year and a half at *Entertainment Weekly* before I left to become an editor at *VIBE* magazine, which was the bible of the urban music world. At this job, I was mostly responsible for polishing other people's work. But on one slow Friday afternoon, I got the biggest shot of my still relatively new writing career.

I was sitting in my cubicle, dutifully counting the minutes before I could leave, when one of the senior editors flew out of her office looking stressed. She stopped briefly in the common area outside my cubicle and I asked what was wrong.

"It looks like the Janet Jackson cover story is going to fall through," she said. "Janet's people need it to happen this weekend, but the writer can't do it."

"What are you going to do?" I asked.

She threw her hands up.

"Can't you reassign?" I offered.

"Of course. But who can we get to do it so quickly? And

it has to be someone we can trust with such a big cover story."

A voice in my mind starting chanting, "I'll do it. I'll do it." The volume grew louder with a force that felt like words were going to thrust themselves out of my mouth. I tightly pursed my lips, trying to lock the words inside. I wanted to say them, but I couldn't. I didn't have the nerve. Sure, I was more skilled at the celebrity interview since my bumbling Mariah days. But still, who the fuck was I? Seriously. Just a little more than a year before, I was selling dick feels for a buck. What made me think I could be a big-time cover story writer? But the voice kept chanting, like the crowd at a football game or a really popular drag show.

The editor stood there thinking for a few moments before she said, "Oh well," and turned to head toward the restrooms.

"I could do it," I said to her rapidly receding back. I winced as the words left my mouth. It felt like I'd just sucked a Lemonhead.

She kept moving.

"I could do it," I said a little louder.

"Huh?"

"I could do it."

She paused. I could see her thinking it over, her expression saying not yes or no but "hmmm."

"You think you could pull it off?" she asked. "Have you ever done a cover story?"

"Uh, well, no. But you know, I did all these big features for the *Washington Post* and everything. And you know,

I've interviewed big stars like Mariah before, so, I mean, yeah, I think I could."

The truth was that despite all the short pieces I'd done at *EW,* the number of long features that I'd ever written added up to about a handful.

"Well, let me think about it," she said.

"Cool," I replied, trying my best to embody the word.

The next few hours went by like decades as I waited for her answer. But then, once she said yes, after getting approval from the editor in chief, time went into fast-forward. The next day I was sitting on a plane to Minneapolis, where Janet was recording her new album, *All for You,* with her longtime producers Jimmy Jam and Terry Lewis. A notebook was on my tray table, and I was thinking up questions for the youngest daughter of one of the most famous black families in the world. There was a lot of ground to cover, considering the recent breakup of her secret marriage to constant companion and collaborator René Elizondo. But the editor had given me only one strict instruction.

"You *have* to ask if she has a secret love child," she said. "The rumor is that she had a baby when she was married the first time to that DeBarge guy and that her sister Rebbie is raising it."

"No problem," I said. "You know I'll ask anybody anything."

"Yeah, I know. That's why you got the assignment."

21

After a couple of hours in the air, my plane landed at the Minneapolis airport around noon, where I was picked up by a chauffeured black town car (a guy even stood in the arrivals section with my name on a sign) and whisked to a downtown hotel. I checked into my suite and proceeded to watch the hotel phone for about five straight hours, moving only once to take a rushed pee. I'd been told that the interview could happen anytime, so I wanted to be ready. But around five, I got sorta hungry and restless, so I went to get dinner at the hotel restaurant. When I got back, the phone's message light was blinking. Damn! It was Janet's assistant letting me know that the interview wasn't going to happen that night after all. She said she'd call to reschedule the following afternoon.

The next morning I woke up and decided to walk around downtown Minneapolis. It was a Sunday morning and the streets were empty and covered with a fresh layer of March snow. I felt really sad, but I didn't know why. All of a sudden this deep lonely feeling came over me. It wasn't the kind of lonely you get when you need a hug or want to get laid. It was more that I felt completely alone with my wants. I wanted—needed—for this interview to work so that it would give me my first cover story, getting me closer to becoming the established entertainment journalist I wanted to be. But I was the only person who could make that happen. Was I going to be able to make Janet like me? Was I going to get juicy quotes out of her? It was so uncertain, I thought as I walked through the virgin snow.

Later that afternoon, around four, the phone rang. It was Janet's assistant, who, oddly, was also named Janet. She told me to go down to the lobby immediately so that I could ride with Janet to the recording studio. I jumped up from the bed, flicked off the TV, brushed my teeth, grabbed my bag, and headed downstairs.

I sat on the couch in the lobby like a TV cop on surveillance, my head turning right and left. Which direction would Janet be coming from? I wondered. I mean, for all I knew, she could sweep down from the chandelier, all dressed in black, a headphone mike around her face, her arms posed in fierce angles above her head. Or maybe some of her background dancers would slink out before her and then she'd suddenly jump from behind a potted plant or something. I simply didn't know what to expect as about fifteen minutes passed by with my mind coming up with increasingly elaborate entrance scenarios. (The front glass shatters, and she comes swooping in like a ninja.)

Finally, I looked in front of me at the bank of elevators and saw that one was open. Inside was a giant of a black man and beside and slightly behind him was a small figure beneath a baseball cap and a shower of golden brown hair. It was Janet.

I walked toward the elevator.

"Hey, I'm Craig," I said. "I think I'm supposed to be meeting you guys."

"Hi, I'm Janet," she said earnestly. It still surprised me when celebrities introduced themselves like there was any chance I wouldn't know who they were. That was cool, though, because no matter what you knew about them, you were still meeting them for the very first time.

I stepped in the elevator and the towering bodyguard pressed the button for the garage. I tried to make small talk. "So, um, how's it goin'?" I asked.

"Fine," she said, not making eye contact.

"Your hair looks nice," I said quickly. I couldn't think of anything else.

"Thanks," she said, trying to be polite. But I knew she was thinking, "Who is this creep?" like I was trying to pick her up at the hotel bar. I wanted to yell out, "No, I'm gay. Totally a fag." But I controlled the impulse.

Once we arrived in the parking area, we walked over toward two black SUVs and Janet told me that she'd be driving the two of us to the studio while the bodyguard followed behind. I went along with the program, got in the car, buckled up, and sat back as she pulled out onto the street. But inside I was worried. I had heard that during interviews celebrities will sometimes try to do normal everyday things like driving in order to appear regular. But this didn't necessarily mean that they were good at the tasks they were trying to pull off. I couldn't stop wondering who had taught Janet how to drive, anyway. Tito? La Toya? Bubbles?

The car moved out from the underground garage onto the street. When we were about a block away from the hotel, the car jerked to a stop and then shot forward. "Oh no," Janet sighed. "I just ran a red light." I looked up from my notepad to make sure death wasn't impending. I was glad that no 18-wheelers were hurling toward the passenger window, but I secretly wished that I had stashed some Dramamine in my bag or maybe even worn Depends. Now, to be fair, I'd certainly run my share of red lights in the past, but I was always more nervous when I wasn't behind the wheel. Plus, the fact that I hadn't decided on my first official question was increasing my anxiety. All of my meticulously prepared questions seemed lame.

I was lost in this thought, as we pulled onto a snow-covered interstate. Sand, salt, and assorted frozen debris splattered against the windshield. "Look at this," Janet said, increasing the speed of the wipers. "Isn't this a mess?"

"Yeah, it's bad," I said, now filled with so much nervous energy that I probably could've propelled the car on my jitters alone. I decided that the only way to ease my nerves was to just start talking. I abandoned my questions and launched into the one topic that made me most comfortable: sex.

"So, you're, like, totally single now," I said. I knew it had been about a year since her divorce from husband René Elizondo had been finalized. "About how many dates does it take before you'll have sex with someone?"

Janet looked over at me with a mix of surprise and amusement.

"Um," she paused. "Well, I really need to get to know a person before anything is going to happen."

"So it's a real-life 'Let's Wait Awhile' situation?"

"You could say that," she answered, giggling.

"What happened the last time you went on a date?"

"Let me try to remember," she said, her eyes scanning the road. "We went to dinner, then we went back to my place. We talked . . ."

"And . . . ?" I asked, feeling much more relaxed now.

"And that was it," she said.

"Really?" I prodded.

"Yes," she exclaimed, laughing.

"OK, OK," I said. Then I decided to tell her a little bit about me and Seth. "So, like, a couple of years ago, I broke up with this guy who I'd been with for a long time, and at first it was weird when I was with other people. Has sex changed for you now that you're single?"

"It's definitely different," she said, alternately glancing at me and looking at the road. "It's never the same as when you're with someone for the first time. That's the part I absolutely love, when there's that newness. There's a little bit of awkwardness that I think is very sexy. But at some point you want someone to call your own." She paused. "But," she continued, "I'm not to that point yet."

"Yeah, after I started dating and, you know, sleeping around and stuff, I started thinking about AIDS a lot more. Do you worry about that?"

"Of course," she said, as we pulled into one of the parking spaces outside the very nondescript Flyte Tyme studios. "But if I let that control my life, I'd probably be celibate, and I don't think I could ever do that. I just enjoy sex too much. But I'm very careful. I try to be as safe as possible and, obviously, not be with every Tom, Dick, and Harry."

"Speaking of 'dick,'" I said, laughing nervously as she turned off the car, "are you a size queen?"

"Honestly, I am." She laughed. "I can't lie. My friends sometimes say, 'You know, Janet, it's not always about the size, but the magic in the wand.' And I'm like, 'But there's nothing wrong with a big magic wand.'"

We continued laughing as we walked to the door of the studio, which—despite being the working home of Jimmy Jam and Terry Lewis, Janet's longtime collaborators and two of the most consistently successful producers in the industry—was located in an out-of-the-way industrial park more suited to an amateur porn operation. We went inside and settled into the studio's lounge. The décor was pretty bare bones, but on one wall was a signed picture of Mariah Carey, who had recently worked with the producers on her new album.

"Oh, my God, Mariah was in *your* studio!" I exclaimed. I'd heard how territorial pop divas could be.

"A lot of people have been in this studio," Janet said with a smirk.

We settled in and sat across from each other at a small table. I clicked on my tape recorder, but left my notebook full of questions in my bag. Our conversation lasted for hours, with topics ranging from growing up Jackson ("No, I've never seen my parents kiss") to her much-discussed weight, which was known for dramatic ups and downs.

"Why do you think people are so obsessed with whether or not you're fat?" I asked.

"Well, my weight *has* fluctuated," she said. "I'm human. But I think the obsession has more to do with them than me."

"Do you think you're sexy?" I figured this was a no-brainer. After all, Janet spent many of her videos dancing around with her often teenager-tight stomach exposed.

"Honestly, I don't," she said without hesitation. "I do not think I'm sexy."

"I don't believe that . . ."

"That's no bullshit," she said. "With God as my witness, I do not think I'm sexy."

"What about when you look at your videos? Do you think the woman on the screen is sexy?"

"No," she answered, her voice getting higher. "I swear to God, no. I don't think she's sexy. She doesn't have it."

"You like sex too much to not think you're sexy."

"I can *feel* sexy. There are times when I'm intimate with someone that I *feel* sexy. But I don't think I *am* sexy. I've never seen myself as sexy. I swear, Craig, I am not lying to you."

"OK, well, everybody masturbates, right?" I asked, trying another angle.

"Right."

"Well, what about when you masturbate? You've got to be thinking you're sexy then . . ."

"Why can't you just be fulfilling a need and getting your rocks off?"

"I guess so. But what in your opinion makes a woman sexy?"

"There's a certain way they move. There's a certain look in the eye. There's a certain something. But it really comes from the inside. It has to be something that the person exudes as opposed to them trying to act sexy. It might be as simple as a smile or the way they walk, the way they carry themselves, how confident they are."

"Are you confident?"

"I don't think I have enough confidence, no," she said, her voice softening. "But it's better than it was. A lot better."

Listening to Janet, I could hardly believe that this international pop icon and sex symbol didn't feel confident or sexy. In a way, I could relate because, growing up as a gay boy, I constantly felt at odds with my sexuality. That's why I'd always admired people like Janet or, say, Madonna, because they appeared sexually powerful. I thought they had the confidence I lacked. But the more I heard Janet talk, the more I began to suspect that almost no one feels fully comfortable with his or her sexuality no matter how they might come across. It seemed like life was just a constant struggle to feel comfortable in your own skin.

With that realization, I eased up on the sexiness stuff and returned to talking about her life as a newly single woman.

"Now that you're dating again, are you ever scared that some guy is gonna be like, 'I just *had* Janet Jackson'?"

"I've been very fortunate so far," she answered. "That's all I can say. I've had guys actually page me and say, 'No one has to know.' Because they understand that that could possibly be a fear and that's what's getting in the way. And maybe that *is* what's getting in the way."

"It must be hard to trust people."

"It's very hard. It's really tough. And everyone needs friends. Everyone needs someone to talk to, to call and say, 'Are you busy? I just need to vent for a moment.' Everybody needs that person in their lives." She paused. "So the question is, 'Who do you do that with?' Or do you hold it inside? And if you hold it inside, how's it going to manifest itself? Who can you cry to without seeing it in the paper the following week?"

As she was saying this, I was thinking about how lucky I was to still have Seth in my life. Despite our differences, I knew that he was someone I could lean on, that I could trust.

"Like I was telling you earlier," I said, "I went through a bad breakup not too long ago, so I know how hard it can be to move on. I was just wondering how you are dealing with it."

"There are times," she said, "when it feels like it just happened yesterday, and there's still a bit of a sting. But I *have* to move on. I have to keep going. I can't let it stress me out, stop me from reaching my goals. I'm just glad that I'm in the state of mind I'm in, because it didn't have to be this way. I could've been one messed-up child. But for some reason, God has put me in a different space. And I'm so appreciative of that. I have to honestly say, 'It's in God's hands.'"

On that note, we finished up because Janet was needed in the recording booth. I was about to put away my tape recorder when I remembered the one question that I was supposed to ask.

"Oh, by the way, do you have a kid?"

She looked at me like I had just farted.

"You know," I continued, "that rumor that you have a kid."

"Oh," she said, understanding where I was coming from, "that rumor keeps resurfacing. They say the kid's in Europe or that one of my brothers or sisters is raising it. But, no, I've never had a child."

I smiled, shook her hand, and thanked her. Mission accomplished.

When I turned in the story, my editor was thrilled with all the talk about big dicks and masturbation. I had succeeded at my first cover story. I knew that I owed much of the success to Janet's willingness to go there with me when I started asking about sex, but I also knew that had it not been for my years at the strip clubs, I probably wouldn't have had the nerve to ask the questions in the first place.

22

Once I'd moved away from D.C., I made it to the strip clubs only a couple of times a year— say, when I was in town visiting family or Seth, who had comfortably settled into being one of my best friends. Every time I returned to the clubs, I was struck both by how different things were—with the no-touching rule still in effect and the influxes of new dancers—and by how much things were exactly as they had been, with many of the same customers sitting in the same places drinking the same drinks, waiting to see that special dancer who they could turn into the boy of their dreams.

One time, just after New Year's in 2000, I was at Wet sipping on a vodka-cranberry. I smiled to myself thinking that I'd worked for years as a stripper before I ever hit the sauce, but now that I was a journalist, I was regularly boozing it up. I was slowly nursing my drink and watching a tan ex-marine strut around the bar, his body like supple granite, when I spotted Dave coming in. I hadn't seen him in more than a year.

"Hey, stranger," I said, motioning for him to take the stool next to me. "Happy Millennium."

"Hey there," he said, walking over. For a moment, we had one of those awkward to-hug-or-not-to-hug moments. Both his arms were slightly outstretched, but since we'd never hugged in the past, it seemed odd to start now. Instead, we transitioned out of this awkwardness with some skillfully deployed back pats, and Dave took his seat.

He asked what brought me to town, and I told him I was visiting friends.

"What about you? What brings you out?" I asked. "The last time I talked to you, it seemed like you were over the whole scene."

"Yeah, well, it comes and goes."

"Seen Peter lately?"

"Not recently," he said with a grin.

"Why are you smiling?"

"Well, you and I haven't talked in a while."

"Did something happen?"

Dave's grin widened dramatically and he told me what had gone down since he and Peter reconnected at the Follies' twenty-fifth anniversary. Not long afterward, Peter started working at La Cage again, and the two of them were back to their regular ritual, sneaking off into corners, Dave working Peter over until he shot his load into a wad of cocktail napkins and breathily sighed over and over, "Oh shit . . . oh shit . . . oh shit."

One night, Dave told Peter that he was about to go on one of his regular trips to New York, to take in the sights and catch a Broadway show, the same thing he'd been doing since the days when he was married.

"Have you ever been to New York?" Dave asked Peter.

"No, I've always wanted to," Peter said, shrugging his shoulders, "but . . ."

"Well, you know, I'd love to have the company if you ever want to go. You just have to let me know."

"That sounds like a good idea, but I'm not sure when I could do it."

"Well, the offer stands and no strings attached. You don't have to do anything you don't want to do. We can get separate rooms and everything if that's what you want. I mean, of course, I wouldn't mind if you wanted to, you know, do 'oh shit.' But you don't have to. The offer stands, so just think about it."

Dave left things there that night, but they kept returning to the topic week after week. Still, Dave told me he didn't really believe it would happen. He deeply hoped it would, but the possibility seemed so remote.

But one night, Peter surprised Dave by saying, "You know that New York trip we've been talking about? I think I would like to do that."

"Now, are you serious about this, because if you are, I'll plan a trip. But you have to be serious about it, because I have to take off from work and make hotel reservations and buy Broadway tickets and it will cost a lot of money. You have to be serious."

Peter convinced Dave that he really wanted to go, and Dave started making plans. Each step of the way, Dave had his doubts. Even as they stood in D.C.'s Union Station about to board the train to New York, he still had trouble believing it was actually happening.

Once they were in New York, everything went as Dave had planned it. They ate at a nice restaurant, took in a show, and Dave even schooled Peter in a bit of gay history by walking him through the West Village, the site of the Stonewall riots, which sparked the modern gay rights movement.

Back at the hotel, they shared the same bed and even did "oh shit." Later that night, Dave fell asleep with his arm around Peter. Dave had finally gotten the intimacy he'd wanted.

"So, are you guys like boyfriends now?" I asked, both a little jealous and titillated.

"No," he sighed, "not really."

Shortly after the New York trip, Peter had to rush back to his parents' house in Rehoboth because his father got sick. But he and Dave would keep in touch by phone a couple of times a month. Dave updated Peter on what was going on in D.C., and Peter told Dave what was going on with his father's health.

"His father got worse with every phone call," Dave told me.

Then one day, Peter called to tell Dave that his father had died. He followed this up with a request that Dave never saw coming.

"I know this is a lot to ask," Peter said, "but do you think you might be able to make it to the funeral?"

Dave felt a mix of emotions—surprise, fear—but he responded simply with, "Of course."

At the funeral, Dave was anxious the whole time and tried to stay on the periphery of things, sitting in the back of the church and not making eye contact with the other mourners so as to not invite questions. But as Peter was escorting his mother out of the church, he introduced Dave as his "friend."

They continued to talk on the phone after that, but the time between calls stretched longer and longer. They hadn't really spent time together or done "oh shit" since New York, and Dave was beginning to think he should move on. There was Jeff, a new dancer and former teenage bodybuilder, who he'd recently turned his attentions to.

"That's partly why I'm out tonight," he explained. "Jeff asked me to help him fill out a job application and I think he wants to use me as a reference."

"What are you going to put under 'relationship'?" I asked.

"I don't know. Family friend," he said, taking another swig from his gin and tonic. "So what about you? Have you found another boyfriend yet?"

"No. Still playing the field, I guess."

He paused. "That's surprising. I always figured you for the type of guy who would settle down."

"Yeah, well. What can you do?"

"You're not getting any younger, you know."

"Thanks for reminding me."

"No. I'm just saying, you don't want to wait too long."

"Yeah, I hear you."

It seemed like everywhere around me people were ready to issue my sexual death certificate. I'd recently had a younger guy I was dating tell me, "I'm just going to go ahead and break up with you now before you're too old to get somebody else, OK?"

So Dave's questions brought the sting of these words back like a fresh slap on a healing wound. After a couple of minutes, I told Dave that I was going to check out what was happening at the other clubs.

"It was great seeing you again," I said, tapping him on the back before making a quick exit. It was the last time I ever saw him.

23

March 2006.

I was riding in a cab through downtown D.C., past the pointy Washington Monument all lit up at night and then down into the tunnel that runs under the Capitol grounds leading to that southeast neighborhood where I'd spent so many nights, most of them naked. The cab was a black-and-orange Capitol Cab like the one my grandfather used to drive. It was another one of those moments that I experienced so frequently in D.C. when my past and present came together in odd and mysterious ways.

I'd come to town this weekend to visit the clubs one last time. Word had come down that the whole block would be bulldozed to make way for a new baseball stadium, the four-hundred-million-dollar centerpiece of a grand plan to overhaul this once-forgotten neighborhood. The clubs had to go because they were, as city officials put it, in the stadium's "footprint." It was unlikely that they would be able to relocate to another part of the city because recent changes in zoning laws made it nearly impossible for sex-oriented businesses to set up shop anywhere else. For a time, it looked like the block's strip clubs, bathhouses, and porn theaters might get a stay of, well, sex-ecution. A judge initially refused to issue eviction notices until the ink was dry on the city's contract with the baseball league. But by late March, the deal was done, and the clubs were given until the first weekend in April to vacate the area that had provided safe haven for more than three decades. The way the whole thing went down echoed, as Hank Stuever of the *Washington Post* described it, "a cruelly predictable high school metaphor: the jocks win."

As soon as I heard about the imminent evictions, I thought about heading down there just to get one last look, to experience the clubs one last time. My life was now so different than it was when I used to scoot across the bar in socks that my grandmother gave me or just hang out in the clubs as a customer. I had changed. The world had changed.

Whenever I reflected on the past five years of my life, I always thought back to an article I was working on in summer 2001. It was a cover story for the now-defunct black women's magazine *Honey* on Lisa "Left Eye" Lopes, the most notorious member of the R&B girl group TLC. The interview took place at an upscale condo in Jersey City, New Jersey. (Sean "P. Diddy" Combs's mom lived in the same complex.) Lopes was staying there while she prepared the release of her debut solo album, *Supernova*.

She felt excited about the project because she thought it would finally allow the world to see her differently—a more thoughtful grown-up rather than the wild child she was when she notoriously torched the house of her boy-friend, NFL star Andre Rison, in an alcohol-fueled rage. She was trying to remake herself. (There was even a black-and-white painting on her bedroom floor with the words "A new star is born.")

"Are you tired of people thinking that you're crazy?" I asked her as we walked along the Jersey City boardwalk at sunset.

"It doesn't make sense for me to fight what people already think," she answered. "I'm not going to run around saying, 'I'm not crazy, trust me.' I can only do what I do. And maybe one day they'll say, 'You know, that girl ain't so crazy, after all.'"

We walked around for a while as the sky grew darker and darker. Lisa had a lot on her mind. She talked about her reconciliation with Rison, who had filled her condo with twenty-six dozen roses that morning and had run out, dur-ing our interview, to pick up some organic vegetables for dinner.

But even in the midst of discussing this current relation-ship, her thoughts kept returning to her brief romance with late rapper Tupac Shakur. According to her, they bonded the moment they met. She was taken by his conversation, music, and charisma; he was drawn to her creativity and piano-playing skills.

Surprisingly, though, they never consummated the relationship. "That's the first thing he told me. 'Never let me have sex with you because I'm going to look at you differently,'" she said. "And I never wanted him to look at me any differently than he did."

"If he'd proposed, would you have married him?" I asked.

"Yeah," she said almost reflexively.

She still thought they would one day be together even though Shakur was dead. "Does that mean I'm going to die in order to be with him?" she wondered. "What does it all mean?"

As it got later and our interview was winding down, we sat on a bench. Lisa started talking about her album again. She was so excited about it that she didn't want to entertain the idea that it wouldn't be a hit. She expected it to sell 20 million copies.

"I'm way too confident, and I realize the power in desiring something and manifesting it," she said. "And I've desired this for so long."

We sat on the bench for a while longer and looked at the Manhattan skyline, which was just beginning to light up. I don't specifically remember looking at the World Trade Center's twin towers but I know they were there. Just a few months later, however, the towers were gone, and the next year, so was Lisa. She was killed in a car accident in Honduras, where she often went to escape music biz pressures.

After her death, I thought about our interview a lot,

what she said about dying in order to be with Tupac and especially the goals she expressed for her album, which was ultimately never released in the United States. Her death was more confirmation of the simple adage that's served up in an infinite number of variations from pulpits all across the world: No one is promised tomorrow.

I started thinking more about my own life—not just what I wanted to do, writing, but how I wanted to live. What kind of life did I want and how was I going to get it? I began making a lot of career moves, transitioning from magazines to newspapers by becoming pop music critic of, first, the *Buffalo News* and then the *Atlanta Journal-Constitution*. But then the daily grind of newspapers started to wear on me. A lot of people imagine it would be fun for your job to entail constantly going to concerts and chasing around celebrities for interviews. But the relentlessness of it made it nearly impossible to have a personal life. Most nights were taken up with shows, and I had to be prepared to drop everything whenever some big music act came to town, got in trouble with the law, or in the case of Lisa, died suddenly. With that kind of schedule, I knew I'd unlikely be able to ever find someone who would fill my apartment with twenty-six dozen roses or buy organic vegetables for me.

All of this made me think about returning to the land of academia. Let's face it, you can't beat the schedule, teaching classes a couple of times a week and having summers off to regroup. I made the decision to return to the University of Maryland to finish my Ph.D., and by the time I heard about the clubs closing, I was living in Providence, Rhode Island, working as a professor in the writing program at the University of Massachusetts Dartmouth, which was about thirty minutes from my apartment. Everything was going great. I loved Providence for its mix of bohemia and working-class grit and, most surprising, I was enjoying teaching.

After years of being a journalist, I now felt I had something valuable to pass on to the students, so I didn't have any of the insecurities I used to harbor about being a fraud. I'd also become much more comfortable with my sexuality and had explored so many facets of it that it didn't feel weird to turn it off and on. I was such a different person than I was when I stripped that I wondered if I really needed to go back to the block. I'd made peace with my time at the clubs—learned from it and, in many ways, thrived because of it.

"Why spend all that time and money just to go back and be sad?" I asked, when I called Seth for his advice. We talked several times a day and people always thought we should get back together. But they didn't understand that we had found a certain peace through friendship, and we didn't want to do anything to trouble the waters.

"You can't pretend it's not happening just because you don't want to feel bad," he said. "There's nothing wrong with being sad about losing something."

"I know, but it feels like I'd be going out of my way just to get all weepy. I already did that when I stopped dancing at the Follies."

"But those clubs used to mean everything to you. I should know," he said, making a dig I tried to ignore.

"So you think I'll regret it if I don't go?"

"I think you need to say good-bye."

• • • Swayed by Seth's argument, I made plans to go to D.C. that very weekend. It was unclear exactly when each club would be closing, and I wanted to be there when they were all still open. It was a little awkward explaining to my parents why I was dropping everything to head to D.C. at the last minute since I still hadn't told them I'd been a stripper. But I simply said I was going to visit old friends, and this seemed true enough.

The cab stopped at the corner of Half and O streets and I got out and went into Secrets. It hadn't changed much since I was last there. I didn't know the guy at the door, but the bartender was still the guy who initially hired me. We shook hands and he made me an Absolut Vanilla with Diet Coke.

I took the drink and made my way through the crowd, which was thick but no more so than on any other Saturday night. I expected to see some signs of the club's impending demise, like sad faces or ghoulish apparitions of strippers from the past twisting and shrieking in the mirrors. But there was none of that. It felt like any other weekend night when people were just out to have a good time.

"Didn't you used to dance here?" said a deep voice coming from my right. I looked over and noticed a short, heavy-set white guy with an eye patch standing next to me.

"A long, l-o-o-o-o-ng time ago," I said.

"You probably don't remember me. I'm Fred."

"Nice meeting you again. Are you here to say good-bye, too?"

"No, I'm not going to say good-bye until the bitter end. Who knows? We might get another week or so."

"Yeah, well, I live out of town so I just decided to come back one last time."

"So, are things the way you remember them?"

"Pretty much. Hey, do you ever see a guy named Michael? He was one of my regulars. He used to love it when I hit him on the head with my dick."

"Oh, yeah. Bald guy? Was always out?"

"Yeah."

"He died a couple of years ago. From what I hear, it was a heart attack. Real sudden. I think he went in his sleep."

"Oh, man. Really?"

"Yep."

"That sucks. I can't believe he died."

"Well," Fred said, "it happens to the best of us."

For a moment, I was shaken. I didn't know how I was supposed to feel. In a way, I didn't know anything about Michael—his last name, his occupation, his survivors if any. But in another way I knew something so singular about him, how he loved getting hit over the head with my dick. What this knowledge ultimately counted for, I wasn't sure. But there was no denying the sense of loss I felt.

"So, have you been to the new club down the street?" Fred asked, mercifully breaking the silence.

"What new club?"

"It's called Heat. It's where La Cage used to be."

I'd forgotten that La Cage had switched ownership about a year before. "Is it worth checking out?"

"Definitely," he said. "It reminds me of the old days before 'The Rule.'"

"Really?"

"Yeah, in fact I'm about to go over there now. I was looking for one boy who was supposed to be dancing here tonight, but apparently he didn't show. Story of my life."

We walked out of Secrets together and I got a stamp so I could get back in without paying again. I wanted to come back because I didn't feel like I'd yet soaked up enough of the atmosphere to last a lifetime. I'd never had a place that meant something to me be demolished. Every other place that I'd moved away from or left behind still existed. I could drive by an old house, apartment, or workplace. But everything on this block was about to be bulldozed. I didn't know how to prepare.

We made our way down the soon-to-be-gone block, past the Glory Hole and the Follies. I kept waiting for some feeling to overtake me, but it didn't come. Nothing felt as meaningful as it should. I wasn't even sad. Instead I was a little tipsy and curious about the boys in the new club.

From the outside, Heat didn't look that different from

the old La Cage, but once I stepped inside, it was a whole 'nother story. Entering Heat was like being dropped in the middle of a porn pajama party. The old club had been gutted so that it was now just one big wide open space like the rec room basement of somebody's parents' house in the eighties. There was one large wooden bar and a makeshift stage that stood about a foot off the floor. All around were dancers, at least twenty of them.

They seemed so different from the guys I used to work with. As a whole, they looked much younger, like many couldn't even legally order a drink at the bar they were dancing on top of, and they also represented a more diverse mix of races than I'd ever seen at a D.C. strip club: black, white, Asian, Latino, and indeterminate. I would've fit in at a place like this. But the most noticeable difference was their attitude. In my day, we tried to make stripping seem like a chore even when we were having a good time. It was very "Look what I have to do to make a buck." But these guys were openly having fun, shaking to the tribal club music pounding from the speakers and talking animatedly to one another and the customers.

As soon as I sat down at the bar, a skinny tan white dancer in bright blue briefs walked over to me.

"I'm Stevie," he said, offering his hand.

"Hey, I'm Craig."

"First time here?"

"The first time since it's been Heat, yeah."

"What do you think?"

"It's kind of wild, but I like it," I said, using my finger

to trace a path down his chest to his smooth belly button.
"What do you do when you're not here?"

"I'm a grad student at Catholic University."

By this point in my life, I'd come to realize that far
from being an anomaly—the grad student stripper—I was
practically a cliché. I'd since met so many other guys, and
women, who put themselves through school by taking off
their clothes.

"Well, here's a donation to the college fund," I said, placing three bucks into his waistband.

"Thanks," he said, moving so close to me that I could
feel the heat of his body.

"How long have you been dancing here?"

"About three months."

"Do you like it?"

"I *love* it. Although I never thought I was the type of guy
who'd do something like this, you know?"

This was another thing I'd come to realize: almost no
one thinks that he is the type of person who would become
a stripper. This is partly because we all want to think of
ourselves as starting out innocent. But it's also because the
very idea of what a stripper *is* exists only in our minds. It's
a fantasy. That's the point.

"I used to be really fat," he continued, "and I used to
hate the way I looked. But working here has been really
good for me. It's the first time I've felt hot."

"Really?" I said, as this dancer basically confirmed all
that I now believed about what made me and so many other
people want to try stripping, that this desire had less to do

with some exhibitionistic impulse than with basic needs that everyone experiences to some degree—to be desired, to feel beautiful, to belong.

"Hey, do you want to do a private?" he asked.

"You guys have private rooms here?"

"Yeah, back there," he said, gesturing to a curtained-off area I hadn't noticed before.

"Maybe later," I said.

"Then I'll be back," Stevie said, before walking away.

"Hey," I said to Fred, who was sitting next to me, "have you ever done a private?"

"All the time. I'm about to get one now," he said, pointing to a spiky-haired twink across the room.

"What happens back there?"

"Depends on the dancer. But things can get pretty wild. I'll give you a full report when I get back."

I nodded, and Fred got up to walk over to the cute punky boy he was looking at. They exchanged some words and then disappeared behind the black curtain.

After Fred left, a young black dancer with a shock of dyed blond hair came up to me.

"Are you having fun?" he asked.

"Sure. You?"

"I'm having a great time," he said, as he put an arm around my shoulder.

"I see."

"That's my goal, to have as much fun as possible."

"Really?"

"Yeah, my sister died last year, and she was like my

mother. And I spent so much time being depressed. But finally I was just like, 'You need to snap the fuck out of it,' you know. So I started working here and I dyed my hair and it's all good."

"What's your name?"

He flashed me a broad white smile. "Mysterious," he said.

We talked for about ten minutes more as he detailed precisely how his sister died, the combination of hair dyes necessary to get his hair to look like it did, and almost everything he did that day from the moment he woke up hearing Mariah Carey's comeback anthem "We Belong Together" playing on the radio. "I love that song so I knew it was going to be a great day," he explained.

Like the other dancer, Mysterious asked me if I wanted a private and I declined again. But I tipped him and he gave me a tight hug before walking away.

Fred came back with a huge grin on his face. Something looked different about him.

"Where's your eye patch?"

"I took it off," he said, moving close to my ear. "It gets in the way of giving a good blow job."

"Wow. I guess you got your money's worth."

"You could say that," he said, climbing back on his seat. I looked for his spiky-haired guy in the crowd, but saw he was already going behind the curtain with somebody else.

"So what are you going to do with the clubs closing?" I asked Fred. "Where are you going to go?"

He frowned. "Me and some of the other regulars have

been talking about it. Some have decided that they are just going to do the escort thing. The only thing about that is you're just sitting home by yourself. The clubs give you someplace to go. But I know this one guy—he's retired—who moved to Florida because he likes one of the clubs down there. And I have another friend who moved to Thailand several years ago after they stopped letting customers touch here. He loves it over there. He used to only like white boys, but he says that after you've been there a while, you barely notice they're Asian."

I wasn't sure what to say to that.

"But," he continued, "I've decided that I'm going to stay put. My health isn't great. I'm on dialysis and my eye is all messed up. I can't really *go* anywhere. But I am going to miss it. Actually, I don't really know what I'm going to do."

While Fred was talking, I spotted a cute curly-haired blond dancer looking at me from across the club. I smiled, he smiled back, and I motioned for him to come over. Fred said something about going to the restroom as I watched the dancer walk toward me. He was tall, with a long, lean body, and he was wearing tightie whities with calf-high white sport socks that had multicolored rings around the top.

"Hey," he said.

"How's it goin'?"

"Good. I've never seen you here before."

"I've never been here before."

We exchanged names—he was Cody, a performing arts

student from Philly. He and another dancer drove down each weekend to work at Heat.

"I guess it lets you put your dance training to good use, huh?"

"You could say that."

"So what's your favorite Broadway show?"

He thought for a moment. "I guess I'd have to say *Godspell*. We did it in high school."

"I'm more of a *Jesus Christ Superstar* guy myself. Judas and Mary Magdalene have some really good songs."

"Yeah, I'm not that into Andrew Lloyd Webber."

"Fair enough. Hey, if I get a private, will you sing for me?"

"What? Are you serious?"

"Yep. I'll totally get a private, but you have to sing me a song."

"What song?"

"Hey, I don't tell a pro what to sing. Whatever you want."

He agreed to my terms and we went over to the back, where a guy took $50 from me and let us behind the curtain into a dark little room with a black leather sofa. I fell back on the sofa as Cody took off his briefs. He then faced me and sat on my lap with his legs straddling me on both sides. He moved his face close to mine.

"So, do you still want to hear me sing, or do you just want to make out?"

"Well, you're totally shorting me. But we can make out if you want . . ."

He pressed his lips to mine, shutting me up in a way that I thought was rude for a second. But only a second. We stayed kissing like this for our entire fifteen-minute time together, as my hands rubbed his back from the nape of his neck to the curve of his bare butt. It wasn't quite sex, but it was sweet, and the best fifty bucks I'd spent in a while. When our time was up, the guy who took the money knocked on the door.

"I guess we have to say good-bye," I said.

"It looks like it."

"I'd say, 'See you later,' but the club is closing in a week or so."

"I know. It sucks."

"Are you going to be dancing anywhere else?"

"I don't really know yet."

"Well, if I ever see you again, you totally owe me a song. Deal?"

"Deal," he said, giving me a hug and one last peck.

I walked from behind the curtain back into the club. It looked pretty empty because it was getting late. Fred seemed to have left and there didn't seem to be any reason to hang around. For a moment, I thought about going back to Secrets one last time, but I decided to leave with the memory of Cody fresh in my head.

I hopped in a cab, and as it pulled away, turning the corner onto South Capitol Street, I looked out of the back window and realized that this was the last time I'd ever see the block as it was. "The last time," I thought, each word feeling heavy, like a boulder.

I imagined that someday families will drive down here on their way to the baseball stadium, and some clean-cut dad will remark how much nicer and safer this area is now that they've cleaned it up. He won't mention all the stripping, porn, and freaky gay bathhouse stuff, but that's what he'll be thinking as he glances in the rearview mirror at his fresh-faced brood. But I know that this wasn't just some wasteland for loners and losers; for many of us, it was where we were most alive.

"So how do you feel?" Seth asked when I called him the next day.

"I don't know," I told him. "I really can't put a finger on it."

It wasn't until a few days later when I was driving through Providence, flipping the radio dial, when a Madonna song came on that summed up how I felt: "This Used to Be My Playground."

24

The first weekend of April 2006 was the last one for the O Street clubs. (Wet got a temporary exemption because it sat a few blocks away, but it closed due to stadium-related development within the year.) Heat issued its last call on Saturday, and the Follies and Secrets/Ziegfield's said good-bye the following night.

According to reports and friends, the vibe at Secrets was sadder than when I was there a couple of weeks earlier. Strippers complained about losing their jobs, and others wondered if they'd ever find another place where they could feel so free. "It's a place where people would come to let go of all their hang-ups and just be who they are," one person told a reporter. "They would discuss deep personal things that they normally kept to themselves, that they don't want anybody to know, to the person sitting next to them at the bar."

Over on the Ziegfield's side of the club, Ella Fitzgerald, in her final show, wiped her eyes and joked about her recent hip problems, telling the packed crowd that she might be making her next public appearance walking with a cane or rolling in a wheelchair. At about 2:30 AM, the lights went down and Ella performed her last number, "The Party's Over," moving her immaculately painted lips to the words: "They've burst your pretty balloon / And taken the moon away / . . . Now you must wake up / All dreams must end."

Morning came a few hours later and found the streets empty. Another chapter of D.C.'s strange gay history had come to a close.

The next morning, Ella, who had a day job as a hairdresser, left her house to get the *Washington Post*, which had done a big story on the closing of the clubs. "I went down to CVS and got like twenty copies," she later told me. "And there was my picture on the front of the Style section. And I just kind of lost it right there by the trash can outside the door. I lost it for about fifteen minutes. I was like, 'Oh my God, it's over. It's gone.' But then I came home, showered, shaved, went downtown, started cutting hair, kept it off my mind, came home that night, read the article, had one more little cry, and then paid it no more mind."

(But even one year after the closing, Ella hadn't completely moved on, especially when it came to the dancers. "I'm still dating one." She laughed. "But he's married now with two kids.")

As for me, I spent much of that last weekend getting drunk in Providence in a sort of inebriated tribute to my past. The funny thing about it is that more than ten years had passed since I started stripping and I still wasn't any closer to having simple answers about why I decided to strip and what the whole experience meant. Whenever someone asked me about it, I wanted to don a solemn expression and break into my take on the *Rent* theme: "One million five hundred seventy-six thousand eight hundred minutes . . . / How do you measure three years in the nude . . . / In hard-ons, in dollars, in dick bites, in porn aud-i-tions."

The thing that made the experience so hard to pin down is that stripping didn't get me any closer to understanding the stuff that I hoped it would. I still haven't figured out why I have this need to see if guys find me attractive, even though their desire often unnerves me as much as it excites me. But at least now I've realized that whatever power I gain from the simple fact that someone wants to have sex with me is too limited and fleeting to be of much use because it has so little to do with me and who I really am. It's all about what I represent to them and how being with me will make them feel about themselves. Whatever they're willing to give up for the chance of sex—whether it's an abundance of flattery or dollar bills stuffed in socks—has to do with their hunger, not my worth. It's nothing I should invest in or stake my value upon.

Yet even while I understand this intellectually, I still suspect that when the time comes for me to check into a gay old folks home, I'll be looking around to see if any guy cricks his arthritic neck my way. I just hope this perpetual need doesn't stand in the way of me finding some kind of happiness.

A couple of years back, I met a guy who made me want to exchange vows. He was a Midwesterner who blushed when he cursed and melted into my body when I held him. We were walking through downtown Atlanta on our way to lunch one day when he told me that despite his feelings, he didn't think we had a future.

"Do you think I'll get bored or something?" I asked. "Or do you think that one guy's attention will never be enough for me?"

He was silent for a while and then mumbled, "I think it's the last one."

I've come to accept that it's just one of my issues— everybody has them—and I'll have to find some way of living with it. But what I know for certain is that stripping is not really an effective way to work out your personal stuff. You can take off your clothes, but your issues cling to you like skin.

• • • "So, what did you learn from stripping?" he asks. I'm back on my date at the bar in Providence, talking to the guy who made me take this excursion through my past. (You know, the guy at the beginning of the book.)

"I don't know," I say, taking a sip of Absolut Vanilla with Diet Coke. "That question is always so hard to answer. I certainly learned a lot about sexuality, and how complex some people's lives are because of it. But I also learned that even in places that you think are all about sex and lust, there are still a lot of people looking for love."

I take another sip. "And as for me, I learned how important it is to take risks, and to go for something no matter what people might think. I mean, those are all clichés I'd heard a million times before, but stripping allowed me to learn it for myself. If I had never been a stripper, I doubt that I'd ever have had the nerve to become a writer or to move around from place to place—D.C. to New York to Buffalo to Atlanta and now to Providence. In many ways, stripping gave me my life."

"So you'd recommend it?"

"Hell no," I say, laughing and almost spraying him with my drink. "I don't think there's anything wrong with stripping, but it's not like my preferred path of enlightenment or anything. Things worked out for me, but they also could've gone badly. I think the point is just to constantly take risks and try to see yourself in new ways. But you don't necessarily have to take your clothes off to do it."

I watch as he processes all of this. I wonder what he's thinking. I'd started the night wanting a kiss more than anything else but I couldn't tell if I was any closer to that goal.

Finally, he looks me in the eye, smiles, and asks if I want another drink.

"Sure," I say.

He gets up and walks to the bar, and I can see from the reflection in the mirror behind the bar that he's still smiling. I might just get that kiss.

Acknowledgments

• • •

This being a memoir, there's a temptation to thank anyone who's ever helped me in life. However, in order to save trees, I will limit my list to those who directly impacted the writing of this particular project. I am deliberately not thanking many people whose stories are included in the book in order to preserve their anonymity. But I do want to acknowledge my friend Lou Chibbaro, whose keen and thorough reporting on gay life in D.C. proved invaluable in researching this book, and "Ella Fitzgerald," who was kind enough to share some memories with me.

Next, I'd like to thank those in the publishing industry who helped bring this book to life: Clarence Haynes, for the conversation that started me on the road to writing this book; Sarah Lazin, for never wavering in your belief in this project; and Malaika Adero, for taking a chance on my story and trusting that I knew how to tell it. Additional thanks go to current and former members of the team at Sarah Lazin

Books: Shawn Mitchell and Danielle McClure, as well
as the staff at Atria Books, particularly Isolde Sauer and
Charles Antony, for taking such care of my "life," Chris-
tine Saunders, for getting the word out about the book, and
Krishan Trotman, for helping me navigate the publishing
process and making sure I had everything I needed.

Thirdly, I'd like to thank some friends and supporters:
Valerie Boyd, for caring enough to go through this with me
once again; Suzanne Van Atten, for always making me feel
understood; Sheri Parks, for so many things over so many
years—I'm in awe of the force you are becoming; Shari
Evans, for being by my side and supporting me throughout
this project and my transition to academia; Biff Warren, for
believing in my vision; and Keota Fields, for being a great
"hanging buddy." Additional thanks go to a few fantastic
writers who I also consider to be friends: David Browne,
Josh Kilmer-Purcell, and Josh Wolk, and to my students
and colleagues at the University of Massachusetts Dartmouth, especially Catherine Houser, the most supportive
chair I could imagine.

Now, I'd like to thank my immediate and extended family for whom much of this book will come as a surprise.
Although you might not understand my journey, please
trust that it is one I had to take. Thanks to Lucinda Moore,
for being someone I can trust—I will always be there when
you need me; my brother, Eric—I want to say "don't make
the same mistakes I have," but instead I'll just remind you
that I'll have your back no matter what choices you make;
my dad, for nurturing every dream I've ever had; and my

mom—the most loving person I know—for giving me the toughness I needed to live life on my own terms.

Lastly, I want to thank three very special guys whose support I counted on through the rough times of writing this book: "Bryce" in Atlanta, "Luke" in Providence, and, most of all, Justin Sirois, for inspiring me and trusting me to be your friend.